Moist-Eyed

Travelogue

Prof Naushaba Siddiqui

Adapted in English
Nisar Akhtar and Asher Noor

Moist-Eyed
© Prof Naushaba Siddiqui 2024

All rights reserved. No part of this publication may be reproduced, stored in a retrieval system, or transmitted in any form or by any means, electronic, mechanical, photocopying, recording or otherwise, without the prior written permission of the author.

ISBN: 9781923163409 (Paperback)

 A catalogue record for this work is available from the National Library of Australia

Cover Design: Asher Noor and Clark & Mackay
Format and Typeset: Asher Noor and Clark & Mackay
Published by Asher Noor with assistance from Clark & Mackay

Proudly printed in Australia by Clark & Mackay

For more information, please contact:
Email: nisar.akhtar.noor@gmail.com
Email: ashernoor@gmail.com
Website: www.ashernoor.com

Dedicated to my grandchildren (born and those yet to come)

Contents

Introduction Asher Noor, Melbourne,
10 February 2024 vii

Foreword Nisar Akhtar, Karachi,
1 January 2015 xi

My Story Naushaba Siddiqui, Karachi,
1 January 2015 xv

Chapter 1 In Search of Minto-E;
From Karachi To Aligarh................................ 3

Chapter 2 In Ghalib's City—Delhi 23

Chapter 3 Aligarh—Two and a Half Days................ 35

Chapter 4 Two Colleges in Agra
and the Taj Mahal.. 51

Chapter 5 Train Journey—Aligarh to
Azamgarh 69

Chapter 6 My Birthplace—
Hasan Manzil, Ghazipur 87

Chapter 7 My Ancestral Village—Pehtia 123

Chapter 8 In the Courtyard
of my Mother's Childhood........................ 139

Chapter 9 Back to Delhi and
Return to Karachi 151

Introduction

Asher Noor, Melbourne, 10 February 2024

This book is the chronicle of a two-week journey in 2014 of my mother, Prof Naushaba Siddiqui, from Pakistan to India. Having migrated to Pakistan around the time of Indo-Pak partition, the journey back after six decades was the culmination of a constant yearning to go back, find her father's grave and take stock of what she had left, or lost, behind.

On the 10th anniversary of her 2014 journey, what you have in your hands is an attempt at translating and adapting the original travelogue from Urdu to English. This was made possible after hours of conversing with her and my father and I adding some more context around the text to make it a more accessible read for the next generation where, English comes more naturally than Urdu. The Urdu version is flawless and flows so well with her command over the language, interspersed with her sentiments penned with intense emotion. This version in

English is partially handicapped because of the inability of English language to capture that raw emotion and furthermore due to my inadequacy to understand and translate the subtlety from the Urdu version.

This is the true story of a journey of an orphaned girl retracing the footsteps of her illustrious elders six decades later. You do not have to have been there at the Indo-Pak partition to acknowledge the magnitude of that loss and the pain. However, with this book in your hands, you can now share in her journey and read how the tribulations gave way to triumph. You will get to witness how she ends up being feted on the trip from those who were strangers to her but who were no stranger to what her forefathers had accomplished.

While the incidents penned in the book will often make your eyes moist, it is more a journey of accomplishments and validation. Once you read this book, you will get a very nuanced insight about the resilience of human spirt, the posterity of good deeds, the role of Divine help and the message that it's never too late.

While all errors and omissions are mine alone, the bulk of the hard work was done by my mother in bringing this book to life. My father provided invaluable addition to both the Urdu and the English versions, and without his steer, we would be rudderless. My brothers chipped in at every crucial stage with input, edits and suggestions to make sure this book sees the light of the day. My wife,

MOIST-EYED

Dr Najia Asher, my unwavering pillar of strength, was my steady supporter and enabler, as I often disappeared into my study for long hours to work on this book. The time it took to write was time away from her and the kids. Their understanding, patience and wholesome support made it worthwhile.

Bon voyage, as you flip the pages, turn the clock and get transported back in time!

***

Asher Noor is the Founder and CEO of his private family office, Odyssey SFO. Before becoming an independent investor and asset manager, he worked for over two decades in the Middle East and Asia in the financial services sector and the private family office world. He is a Fellow of the Institute of Chartered Accountants of Pakistan, Chartered Institute of Management Accountants UK and of the Family Firm Institute USA.

He has been on the board of multiple companies (both in the private and public domain) in sectors as diverse as aviation, education, contracting, energy, F&B, financial services etc.

He has served on several publication committees and editorial boards, including the prestigious STEP Journal. He has an MBA from EDHEC Business School, France.

Asher has spoken at over 50 global conferences and has multiple publications to his credit.

A lifetime member of the Arts Council of Pakistan, an avid bibliophile and cricketer, Asher is now based in Melbourne, Australia.

Foreword

Nisar Akhtar, Karachi, 1 January 2015

When Naushaba entered my life and our home as my newlywed wife, she brought with her, among other worldly possessions, a sizeable envelope that held immense significance for her. The contents of this envelope were aged papers, tinged with yellow, on the verge of crumbling, and almost decaying, with missing corners and fading ink. While I initially assumed they possessed historical importance, I soon discovered their true value lay in sentimentality. Alongside this collection of papers were two diaries that had once belonged to her late father, Hasan Abdullah. These diaries represented her sole connection to him, as they were inscribed with his own handwriting. Despite being orphaned at an early age and having limited memories of him, she could effortlessly recognise his penmanship from among a stack of hundreds of handwritten pages.

Among the collection, there was another book that held a special place in her heart, *Ganjaha-e-Granmaya* by

Prof Rasheed Ahmed Siddiqui. This particular book featured a chapter dedicated to her late father, who left the mortal world in haste.

More cherished than any jewellery or other worldly possessions, she safeguarded these precious papers in a secure drawer within our cupboard. Remarkably, even after four decades have passed, only she remains privy to the location of the key to that drawer.

The content of those papers has been narrated to me countless times. Naushaba draws her strength from the words inscribed on those papers—press clippings, publications, manuscripts, letters and more—that bear witness to her family's illustrious legacy. Her joy and sorrow have consistently been intertwined with those pages. However, this doesn't imply that she dwells solely in the past. Her present is impeccably managed. She has successfully raised five wonderful children, and her ability to balance both her professional and family life is undeniable. Those who come to know her and her story are consistently in awe of her adeptness. This remarkable juggling act has persisted for over four decades. She clings steadfastly to the lives, accomplishments and legacy of her elders as if they were prized and well-deserved possessions.

The upheaval brought about by the Indo-Pak partition and the subsequent migration certainly turned her

MOIST-EYED

life upside down. Despite this, she has always believed in destiny and in making the best of the cards dealt to her.

With these historical family papers, Naushaba meticulously crafted *Kamal-e-Hasan*, an eloquent testament that chronicles the life stories of her forefathers. Through *Kalaam-e-Ashraf*, she artfully compiled a collection of her grandmother's poetry. Yet, her ambitions extended beyond the written word. Desiring to retrace the footsteps of her elders, she embarked on a journey to visit the places in India they had once called home—places that, by virtue, should have been her home as well. In India, she emotionally poured her heart out, and if one were to quantify all those tears, they could perhaps fill up a lake.

Upon her return, the tears did not cease. She passionately recounted every moment of her emotional journey to me. Now, that very journey rests in your hands in the form of a book, aptly titled *Chashm-e-Nam*.

Keep a handy supply of tissues nearby, for shedding a tear or two is inevitable as you delve into this book.

This is the enchanting yet genuine life story of an orphan who, from a tender age, courageously faces all challenges to skillfully unearth and reconstruct the path of her elders in a foreign land from a bygone era.

***

PROF NAUSHABA SIDDIQUI

Mr Nisar Akhtar, born in 1941, graduated from University of The Punjab, Lahore, with Masters in Statistics and Economics. He obtained another master's degree from the State University of New York at Albany (SUNYA). In addition, he holds a LLB degree from the University of Karachi, Pakistan. He joined the Statistics Department of State Bank of Pakistan in 1962, rising to the position of Additional Director at the Bank, at the time of his retirement in 2001. He is also an alumnus of the prestigious IMF Institute, Washington.

Post retirement, he has pursued his literary interests and honed his passion for calligraphy. He is an active member of the Arts Council of Pakistan, Karachi, and also a life member of the Aligarh Muslim University Old Boys Association (AMUOBA), Karachi. He is presently associated as a convenor at the Dr Jameel Jalibi Research Library at University of Karachi.

My Story

Naushaba Siddiqui, Karachi, 1 January 2015

Travel is the conduit to prosperity—truer words have never been spoken!

After migrating from my birthplace in India to my forever homeland Pakistan, during the time of Indo-Pak partition, my first return trip from Pakistan to India has certainly left me with an unimaginable liveliness and an immeasurable richness in the heart.

For more than six decades, I had longed to visit my birthplace and ancestral homes. The yearning was to wander through those streets, neighbourhoods, villages, towns and cities, where my elders had lived and breathed amidst those dwellings that they had called their very own. The desire was to marvel at the mansions they had built, inhabited and then had to leave behind, retracing their steps and navigating the roads they would have regularly commuted. I wanted to relive those seasons they would have weathered. I wanted to immerse myself in those schools, colleges and universities where they had shined and outshined. I wanted to clock in hours at places where they would have worked and to bow my head in mosques where they would have shed tears while earnestly praying for my prosperity. All in all, I had always believed that I would find consolation in revisiting and rediscovering my birthplace and ancestral homes—even though I have lost them all.

A century is a long time, from when my elders lived and then let go of all those places in India. I was not sure what, if anything, would have remained of those neighbourhoods, buildings, people and their accomplishments. Could it be that some of it still remained preserved and revered, or had all been lost in the sands of time?

With no one in my immediate circle from that era alive to inquire of, maybe my journey would provide me these answers.

What I feared most was discovering how no effort was made to save the treasure trove of books, writings and private libraries.

What I feared most was finding out that our personal belongings, which had immense sentimental value, had been chucked out without any cause, concern or care.

What I feared most was witnessing once-fertile farms reduced to barrenness, gardens uprooted, and wells dried up.

MOIST-EYED

The Indo-Pak partition of 1947 undeniably deprived me and my family of much, exacting a heavy toll that we continue to bear.

Nevertheless, the sacrifice made by millions for the cause of independence, including myself, was a profound and meaningful one. I take pride in being part of the generation that could secure Pakistan by relinquishing everything else. The gift we leave behind for our children—which is Pakistan—is unparalleled, and there is no better legacy for them to cherish and nurture.

Despite the apprehension gnawing at my conscience, the desire to embark on the journey to India persisted. I longed to witness firsthand the aftermath and consequences of historical events.

My heart ached to witness the walls of Halima Manzil and step into the halls of Muhammad Ali Manzil. The very thought of peering down the well in my ancestral village tugged at my emotions. Regardless of the current owners of my ancestral lands, I yearned to witness them—lush green and thriving, ideally. The desire was to inhale the fragrance and relish the sounds of my ancestral city, my birthplace. Crossing the thresholds of Hasan Manzil and Samad Manzil, inherited by my father from his father, who in turn inherited them from my great-grandfather, was a pilgrimage I longed to undertake. Though the rightful inheritance was meant for me and my siblings, I had reconciled with the reality decades ago that it had slipped away into the hands of strangers.

Visiting the educational institutions where my elders learned to read, write and eventually became the shining stars they were held a special place in my heart. Furthermore, I yearned to explore the centres of learning that they in turn had funded and built.

For a long time had I harboured a modest dream—to travel the corridors of the past. However, this aspiration remained elusive for far too long. The primary culprit was the constraints imposed by my government service in Pakistan, compounded by the persisting cross-border conflicts between India and Pakistan. These geopolitical challenges consistently stalled any endeavours to embark on the journey to India. Furthermore, there existed the additional complication of my children either being too young, navigating crucial stages of their educational journeys or getting married. These formidable milestones requiring my presence with them effectively imprisoned my desire, preventing any substantial strides towards the Indian odyssey.

Alternatively, it occurred to me that perhaps I was blissfully unaware that my destined journey was predetermined only for the year 2014 and not a moment sooner.

On 14 April 2014, as I celebrated my youngest son's wedding, a realisation dawned upon me—it was now or never. The time had come for me to carve out a space to live for myself, even if only a little bit.

On my birthday on 24 April, a date that typically marked another year passing without the opportunity

MOIST-EYED

to ever having visited my father's grave in India, I took a decisive step. Gathering whatever documents I could muster; I submitted my application for an Indian visit visa. Living in the shadows of the past had become a familiar routine, but on that fateful day, something within me shifted. I acted on the dream I had always harboured but never actualised before.

The night preceding my visa application, a somewhat spectral symphony unfolded. I heard my father's voice resonating from the Aligarh Muslim University graveyard, my grandfather's call echoed from the Hasan Manzil of Ghazipur, and my great-grandparents beckoned from Samad Manzil and Muhammad Ali Manzil. The experience was surreal; I could tangibly feel the energy and the resounding calls directed towards me. Overwhelmed, even the most basic sights, like the courtyard of my mother's house, fuelled my enthusiasm. Unable to contain myself, I woke up with an urgent determination, and armed with whatever scant documentation I could manage, I promptly submitted my application for an Indian visit visa.

Yet, even with this newfound determination, I held no delusions of a favourable outcome for my visa application. The telepathic summons had ignited my resolve, but the formidable challenge of persuading the Indian visa officer loomed large, fuelled by the persistent worry that my limited documentation might fall short. With the application submitted, I found myself once again navigating the corridors of the past. Tears of helplessness shattered the patient barriers I had built over decades. Immersed in an ocean of tears, I envisioned my father beckoning me from his final resting place in the Aligarh Muslim University graveyard, turning my thoughts to his extraordinary legacy.

My father, Hasan Abdullah, a distinguished student of Aligarh Muslim University, who then took over the role of an esteemed employee, lay buried in the expansive university graveyard, a privilege that was accorded to him as a mark of respect and honour. Renowned for his impeccable dressing sense, his intellect, personality and capabilities were revered by all.

During World War II, grappling with the challenges of managing limited finances and rationing needs, Aligarh Muslim University sought an exceptionally honest and capable individual. Without hesitation, they turned to my father. Although he had applied for a teaching position, they astutely declared, "We might find a good professor, but an able steward is impossible to find." Consequently, he had been appointed as the Steward of Aligarh Muslim University. This unparalleled honour is eloquently chronicled by Prof Rasheed Ahmed Siddiqui in his seminal work *Ganjaha-e-Granmaya*.

More than half a century later, I found myself handicapped without a visa, betraying the persistent calls from my late father to come and find his resting place. Anticipating a delayed or denied ruling from the visa offi-

MOIST-EYED

cer, life unfolded in a manner more fantastical than fiction. Exactly four days later, on 28 April 2014, I held in my hands my Pakistani passport, now stamped with a three-month visit visa. This remarkable turn of events opened an unbelievable opportunity for me to journey to India and pay my respects at my father's grave.

The sheer luck and fortune I encountered, and the swift unfolding of events in a matter of days, left me in disbelief. The unthinkable had transpired with unbelievable ease and speed.

Upon receiving the visa, my immediate thought was that it must be a Divine calling that had prompted me to take action. I pondered why it took over sixty years for my father's spirit to beckon me. I questioned what delayed my ancestral homes, villages, farms and the seasons from across the border in extending their invitation for so long. Regardless, the time had finally come for the journey of a lifetime, and without a moment's hesitation, I seized the opportunity.

On 19 May 2014, I boarded a PIA Airlines flight from Karachi, Pakistan, and remarkably and unbelievably, it departed and arrived in Delhi, India, precisely on schedule. With a three-month visit visa that spared me the obligation of daily reporting to the local police station, I found myself unburdened and devoid of stress.

Despite my tentativeness, I had booked a two-week trip with a return ticket, assuming it would be sufficient to explore my ancestral places—or whatever fragments remained of them. As I traversed through the ruins of ancestral homes, barren farms, dried-up wells, and unfamiliar streets, I anticipated no grand welcome. Responding to a call from the grave and propelled into action, I did not anticipate a jam-packed itinerary.

In retrospect, those two weeks raced by, proving woefully inadequate for the reception that awaited me. Each day, I spent hours crouched next to my father's peaceful resting place in the Aligarh Muslim University graveyard. The university, where my father had once commanded such respect, embraced me with an honour, regard and warmth beyond my wildest imagination. My sheer pride of seeing my great-grandfather's name engraved on the Aligarh Muslim University entrance door unrivalled any glory I could have ever dreamt of.

Witnessing the remnants of Hasan Manzil and Samad Manzil unleashed a torrent of tears, as I struggled to offer feeble justifications to the barren lands that once thrived under our ownership. It felt as if they were reproaching me, questioning why it took me so long to come and see them. Our orchards, once brimming with mangoes, guavas, water chestnuts, melons and other fruits, now stood desolate. The 200-year-old water well had run dry, seemingly dried out while crying in our memory. The tears from my eyes that I poured into the well became the only drops it had collected in a long, lonely time.

The silence within Hasan Manzil was deafening; I, the inheritor of this place, had taken my first steps in its courtyard. Goats and chickens once roamed there freely and were named after me and fed by my hands. Hasan Manzil likely bled tears at this long-awaited reunion, staining my heart with the profound realisation of loss. The courtyard of my mother's house, witness to the prime of her youth, served as a poignant reminder of my maternal grandparents.

I became a tourist in my own home, in my own village, in my own cities. I captured those poignant moments in both my memory and digital form, the latter primarily for my children and grandchildren. It was my attempt to anchor them to their roots, even if they never get a chance to set foot on the soil I tread.

The return journey to Pakistan felt like returning to a nation of aged individuals, where the young generation had flown the coop, seeking opportunities and flights to distant continents. We, who had sacrificed everything for the dream of independence, found ourselves facing yet another exodus, merely a generation later.

As I live out my days in borrowed time, the senior citizens of Pakistan yearn for the next visit from our children, while missing our grandkids even more. We dream of their growth, their struggle with learning Urdu in distant lands and their appreciation of their heritage. Despite knowing that I won't witness it, I am confident that someone from the generations beyond will embrace the past, the pedigree and the ancestry. They will dust off this book, decades from now, read, enjoy and feel proud of who we were and what I have documented. What I write now is for that child of mine in the future.

I often wonder if that child will shed a tear reading this story. It's a question I pose to myself every day, a question that holds immense importance for me. Some of the content in this book may not be as thrilling for others, but it means the world to me. It encapsulates my family's personal journey, and I believe there is no better way to preserve that memory than in the form of a book for generations to come.

1

When the intensity of sorrow peaked, the signals of happiness began to overpower the grief. Tears welled up in my eyes, yet my mind was doing its own manoeuvres. I was trapped in a mind–body state situation.

Chapter 1

In Search of Minto-E; From Karachi to Aligarh

Life is a tough balancing act between priorities—where some compete for attention, and others demand more resources.

    This is not just what life but also what Economics teaches us. I have been a student and teacher of that subject all my life. Whenever I used to explain this concept to my students, I used to realise that my wishes too have always remained beholden to the competition between resource availability and desires. However, over time, I have come to the realisation that there is a bigger principle in play called Divine will. Availability of resources alone cannot make all desires come true. They need the blessings of the Almighty as well. That is why, to-date, despite having the resources, my biggest wish since birth had remained unfulfilled.

    My foremost wish had been to visit the places from pre-partition India that my elders once called their own. I wanted to retrace their steps, immerse myself in their storied past and come face to face with their illustrious legacy. It was their legacy that had been a perpetual source of inspiration for me while helping me navigate the challenges of life.

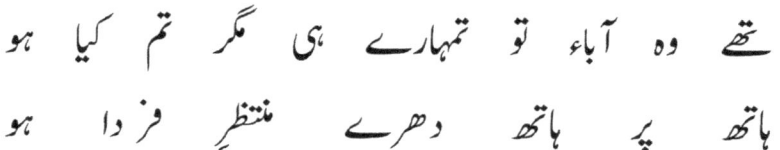

*Glory be to your forefathers indeed, but what of you;
Fruitlessly whiling away time, waiting for manna.*

While it's good to reminiscence of one's elders and take pride in their accomplishments, the more imperative thing is to emulate them. I am not sure I accomplished as much as them, but I have strived and always taken pride in all their accomplishments, and they seem to have inspired me every day of my life.

I was now fortunate to be visiting places where, while their footprints might have disappeared, my heart still resonated with the echoes of their presence and my eyes could vividly paint images of their existence. I was going to get to step into the imprints left by my forefathers, much like a child donning their parents' shoes as they learn to walk. Big shoes impede easy movement at first, but getting up after every fall and taking the next baby step forward finally

MOIST-EYED

makes the child gain the confidence to be able to stride comfortably in those big shoes without falling.

I remember that when I was very small and got new shoes, after taking a few steps, I would take off my shoes, look at the soles and cry that they were now dirty. My family used to gather around and try to console me. Some stated the soles were meant to get dirty, while others suggested cleaning them. However, I persisted in my tears, refusing to believe they could be restored, since they were now dirty.

It was then that my most treasured relation ever would pluck me from the ground and in whose arms I would feel most comfortable. He would give away the shoes to a nearby maid, and a clean pair would soon appear for me. This would happen almost every other day. I never forgot to cry, and that treasured relation never disappointed me, for invariably and inevitably, a new pair would appear. He used to say to all those who criticised that I will understand when I grow up, and in the meantime, if we end up buying a few more shoes, so what. He used to say that Allah had given us the resources and means to buy a few more pairs, and in this trade, if the kids of our maids end up with a few extra pair of new shoes—along with his daughter—this was not a bad bargain.

Yes, this was my father in whose lap I found the best comfort and sanctuary in the world, oblivious to how the real world worked.

It was not long thereafter that this lap was lost to me forever. Somehow, I also instantly stopped crying and insisting. It seemed to all that I had grown older and wiser with this loss. It soon became evident to me, though, that no happiness lasts forever. If you find it, hold on tight to it while you can. If you don't find it, don't cry for it, because that is what Divine will is all about. I never blamed Allah for the loss of that lap, but I always asked that question to myself, "Why me?" Not every question has an answer. It was not like the compulsory question in the exam paper for which I had to necessarily find an answer.

I kept finding answers to all the riddles in life, until the desire to revisit my ancestral land resurfaced. I wanted to follow the footsteps of my elders, despite them being beyond the border. I wanted to walk in those footsteps, even if they had been dimmed or destroyed by the decades. The desire and resources had always been there, but the destiny had chosen 19 May 2014 when I was to fly out to my ancestral land for the first time, with the visa allowing me to go ahead and fulfil my ultimate desire, albeit more than half a century too late.

In this time period, I had lost out on many who had kindled my love and desire for my ancestral place while regaling and reminiscing tales of those times. It was now up to me to get to the climax of this unfinished novel.

The plane from Karachi to Delhi was up in the air, and the airhostess was informing in her typical monotone

MOIST-EYED

the expected flight details. Who hasn't heard the saying, "*Hanooze Dilli Duur Ast*" (Yet Delhi is far away), but Delhi was a mere two hours away. Those two hours went by in a flash, or so it seemed, given my preoccupation with my mixed emotions and thoughts.

Everyone knows of the historical importance of Delhi. However, during the flight, I did not recall Lal Qila, nor the Jamia Masjid minarets, no Qutub Minar came to mind, and neither did all the other achievements of the Mughals as carved in red stones around the city. My thoughts were imagining the old Delhi train station and the regular commute of my father between Aligarh and Delhi. I was wondering which road he would have taken, which platform he would have stood at, which railway porter would have helped him with the ticket and luggage.

The plane landed on time, and immigration was a breeze courtesy my airport porter. Soon thereafter, I had ended up at Orient Hotel, room number 23.

I still could not believe that I had actually crossed the border for which I had been waiting all my life.

I decided to step out of the hotel for a walk. In an unbelievable trance, I crossed the step stairs of the Jamia Masjid, where the prayer mats for congregation were laid out on the floor and people were praying. Those who were praying were obviously collecting rewards for their virtue, but I also marvelled at the foresight of those who had contributed to building the mosque with their money or skills and how they would be earning rewards daily as well, long beyond their lifetime, for their efforts that had led to an edifice from whose pulpit until the Day of Judgement, the words "Allah is The Greatest" will resonate.

I saw a pile of tiles and bricks that seemed to have fallen off the walls of the mosque and just swept into a pile in a corner. I captured that in a click. I was asked why I had bothered to click them when the majestic arches of the mosque provided for a more fascinating photograph. I replied that I had seen those arches in many books, but nobody seems to marvel at the fallen bricks and tiles. They are like the fallen leaves, dead and departed, soon forgotten, just like our own dearly departed. I have usually swum against the tide and thus doubt if my answer found any acceptance.

In Delhi, I got to see the Lal Minar, Qutub Minar and many other buildings that displayed the creative and architectural genius of the Mughal dynasty and have given a perpetual lease of life to Mughal architecture.

I also got to visit Nizamuddin Aulia's Aastana. There were devotees everywhere. They were in a state of ecstasy or frenzy and did not seem to be aware of their own physical body or this world. For a while, I too got spellbound into that state of mind and trance myself. On my way back to the hotel, I kept on thinking that my forefathers too would surely have spent considerable time visiting this Astana. I had thankfully trod carefully at the shrine, for while our eyes cannot see the footprints of the past, they are nonetheless there, and I did not want to disturb them.

MOIST-EYED

On 21 May 2014, I hired a car and a driver and began my journey to the destination that was my primary draw - Aligarh Muslim University. Throughout the ride, I was in a world of my own. I was cleaning my glasses every now and then, for my teary eyes were getting cloudier with each passing moment.

I had started talking to these roads. Despite the bizarre profound sadness, there was also an inexplicable joy bubbling within me. When the intensity of sorrow peaked, the signals of happiness began to overpower the grief. Tears welled up in my eyes, yet my mind was doing its own manoeuvres. I was trapped in a mind-body state situation for which the poet has rightly said:

یہ میرا چمن ہے میرا چمن، میں اپنے چمن کا بلبل ہوں

سرشارِ نگاہِ نرگس ہوں پا بستۂ گیسوئے سمبل ہوں

This is my garden, my very own garden, and I am its nightingale;
That's me—hooked on the poet's narcissus;
bound by the tresses of the hyacinths.

Soon, I was inside the perimeter of the hallowed Aligarh Muslim University, my alma mater in spirit and by association. I had lived on the campus as the young princess—the toddler who had daily demanded and duly received new shoes. It was somewhere here that my safe sanctuary, the affectionate lap of my father, was forever lost so early on for me. It was somewhere in this air that my father's voice, which used to nourish me with bedtime stories, was lost for eternity. It was in this university's graveyard that my universe lay buried. More than six decades had elapsed in my daily yearning for that proximity. And now, I was here!

It was while putting down my luggage in the university's guest house room number 7 that I suddenly felt a chill pass through my body. I was electrified. It had been such a long, arduous wait; however, I was finally here. The synchronization of the lining up of desires, resources and the Divine will had well and truly happened. It could not have been possible without the blessings of Allah. I felt eternally grateful.

The first thing I did as I unpacked was to take out my book *Afkar-e-Hasan* from my bag. My life flashed by me in an instant. I had gone from an infant to a little daughter, who got orphaned, to a student, to a wife, to a mother, to a grandmother—my take on the Shakespearean seven stages of life. Out of the 24 hours that make up my daily life, I had dedicated an overwhelming 25 hours daily to serve my college students in my professional role and my family members and their needs in my domestic roles. However, today marked a momentous occasion, as I was there in my own world, solely for myself.

It was 48°C outside. Such unbearably heat that even the eagle would leave its nest. Undeterred, I stepped out of the guest house and asked around for directions to the

MOIST-EYED

graveyard. It was not normal walking distance, but distances did not matter anymore. *Afkar-e-Hasan* was in my hand as I briskly walked towards the general direction of the graveyard. Soon, my throat was parched. My feet were burning and hurting. The road seemed to be breathing fire. However, the temperature meant nothing to me, despite scorching my body. My heart was pounding. What gave me momentum though was this verse in my mind:

ان راستوں میں دفن ہیں میری خوشی کے پھول

On these roads are buried the flowers of my happiness.

Somehow, I defied the distance and the heat and reached the graveyard. A board on the side of the entrance, instructed those arriving, of the prayer one should make before entering the graveyard.

I stopped, caught my breath and gathered courage, and instructed my tears to stay put. However, as Mir had said:

پاس ناموسِ عشق تھا ورنہ
کتنے آنسو پلک تک آئے تھے

Were it not regard for the dignity of love;
Score of tears stayed put at the eyelids.

In the graveyard, I was stopping at each grave, trying to read the headstones to find my father's grave. I started shedding tears and possibly cried more than I had ever cried in my life.

On an unbearably hot afternoon, here was a luckless daughter who had arrived after more than six decades of yearning with the sole objective of finding the final resting place of her father. Here was a daughter who only had the faintest recollection of the face of her father, seen otherwise mostly through his few photographs that had survived and known mostly through the writings he left behind or through people who had been fortunate to spend more time with him than she had been and had anecdotes to share.

Getting to and finding that two-yard plot in the ground in this graveyard is what had consumed me all of my childhood and adult life. However, now that I was almost there, in the same graveyard as my deceased father, it was still not proving to be an easy or magical end to a long-awaited reunion. Grave after grave, my quest seemed never-ending and unyielding. I could not find my father's final resting place.

Was my father playing hide and seek with me? Maybe he was having fun and enjoying this?

I was stopping at each grave, cleaning up the headstone to read the text and then moving onto the next in despair mixed with anticipation. The elusive headstone

MOIST-EYED

had yet to make itself known to me. With each passing minute and headstone, something in me was dying, and I was getting extremely disheartened.

What if my father was not playing but instead punishing me for taking so long to come see him?

I spent several hours in the failed search. It felt like a century. Tears had long dried up. The heat and my feet were killing me, but that had not slowed me down. The dust on the soles were the least of my concern, especially when I was drenched in sweat and dust all over. Shrubs had scratched and pierced through my feet, and blood too had caked on my feet, ankles, hands and elbows. I had almost given up hope for that miracle but wasn't willing to slow down or give up.

The gist of the landmark article *Umeed ki Khushi* by Sir Syed Ahmed Khan kept playing in my mind. Never lose hope. I had learned this mantra in my primary school and had successfully clung to it as my guiding light all along.

Exhausted, I then cried out loud, "Where are you, Baba? I have come from so far away, just to meet you. I am six decades late, but hey, at least I am finally here. Please see me."

The tides of time had grown sturdy shrubs on the graves, masking the inscriptions on the headstones that were layered with dust. It could not be flicked away easily. A few passers-by had come around to aide my quest as well. Everyone tried to find the elusive grave. None succeeded in helping me find my father's last abode.

With a sinking heart, as I walked the long stretch back to the guesthouse, an infidel thought rang out in my mind. "Oh Allah, first you took him away from me when I was merely an infant, and even now, you have made his grave invisible and him unavailable to me. Is this fair? Is this just? Why?"

I, however, soon returned to my senses, apologised to Allah and reinforced my solid belief that everything happens for a reason, and there is a time and place for everything. That night, I decided that I would return as soon as day light broke the next day so that I could have the whole day ahead of me to start the quest afresh at the graveyard.

It turned out to be a dreadful night for me.

They say when we sleep, we almost embrace death. That is why when we awaken, we should thank Allah for giving us another shot at life. I tried to get some sleep, but my mental faculties were still in full swing. I seemed to be talking to myself non-stop while picturing that somewhere not too distant from my guesthouse, my father rested in his perpetual sleep. This was the shortest physical distance that I had been to him in over six decades, and yet, I hadn't found him. Despise the Aman Ki Asha (Hope for Peace) initiative that had rekindled my desire and made the journey possible, it seemed some distances still could not be bridged.

MOIST-EYED

In the morning, during Fajr prayer, I feverishly sought and repeated for that one wish to come true. All my life, I have always had a lengthy wish list for the Almighty that sought blessings for each member of my family, friends and relatives. Today, I only had that one wish to come true. As soon as it was morning, I was back on the long trek to the graveyard. I had resolved that today, nothing was going to prevent me from finding my father.

I stepped into the graveyard from the iron-gate side entrance. Inside, on the right side was the mosque. On a whim, I decided that I was going to start from the right-hand side. The headstone inscriptions, though, were facing the other way. Unless I got to the end of the wall, I could not see that side of the headstones with the inscriptions. Finding a small, barely manageable walkway, I nonetheless charted my way through. Now, while I could see the headstones, but they were all clad in layers of dust and required cleaning to barely let me make out the name of the occupant of the grave. This was an extremely time-consuming, laborious and tough task and was yielding nothing. I went back and forth, but soon, I lost all measure in the sheer hopelessness of the situation and started crying.

I stood amidst the dead and addressed them aloud. "This is not fair, Baba. I came yesterday. I have come again today. Seems like you don't want to meet. I will leave day after tomorrow. Is this fair? Since the time I could understand and recollect things, you came here and hid. I waited for you all my life. And now when I am here, you are still not going easy on me. This is not fair baba." I was crying and hysterical. "I have come from very far away. Please meet me, Baba. Please, Baba. Please."

Rafiq, the graveyard caretaker, had heard my wailing and came about. He had seen me in my desperation yesterday as well. I briefly told him my story, and despite living among the dead, he immediately understood my pain. His prayers joined my prayers in the mission to find my father's final resting place. It then seemed to me as if someone whispered in my ear, "I am here. Come."

Exhausted, I had just sat next to a grave. There were many shrubs on that grave. The headstone had almost gone black. The grave was caked in dust. As if through some Divine instruction and nudging, I started to peel the dust away with the tissues I was carrying for this very task. Slowly, a name started to partially reveal itself from beneath the decades of layers of dust, but the partial name reveal was more than enough for me. I shrieked in a mixture of disbelief and extreme happiness. I doubt if anybody would have ever screamed so loudly in that graveyard.

I had finally found that two-yard plot of land where the Steward of Aligarh Muslim University, favourite student of Rasheed Ahmed Siddiqui and the famous personality of *Ganjaha-e-Granmaya*—Hasan Abdullah—my father, lay asleep.

MOIST-EYED

Here lies the son of Molvi Abul Hasan, who himself had an illustrious pedigree and track record from Indian Education Service and member court of the Aligarh Muslim University, secretary to Nawab Waqarul Mulk, in-charge duty society and as director education of the Kashmir estate.

Here lies the young man, my father, who had left an indelible mark on so many and yet left the world at the young age of 40 years.

The sun was out and scorching. However, I was focused elsewhere. I was finally in my father's company. The yells had given way to stunned silence as I kept looking at the headstone, which I had fully cleaned up with my tears. Getting here had been my life's foremost dream. Today, that dream had finally come true. It seemed to me that from hereon, there was nothing else left to yearn and quest for. I had found my paradise.

To the side of the grave, I placed the book *Afkar-e-Hasan*, as if it was some library shelf. I had compiled this book by collating my father's writings and extracts from some of his diaries that I had been fortunate to access over the years and had clung onto dearly. The book, to me, was the solitary, possibly lone yet inconsequential, act I had done for my father ever, for I never had a chance to do anything else for him—like giving him a glass of water, pressing his legs or helping him with his shoes. I only learned to have memories or read and write when he had already left this fickle world. I had compiled his writings from the ones I was able to retrieve from family members and had published them, fearing lest they be lost in the sands of time. For years, I had wanted to bring his book to him, but the tensions at the border had delayed this. That border did not exist when he had passed away so young, so suddenly.

I have always wondered how many other writings of his I was deprived of because of the partition. We lost everything in that partition, and yet, I am of the generation that believes that what we got in the bargain was worth the sacrifice. We had not been forced to migrate. We had taken it upon ourselves to migrate, because the cause was bigger and worthier.

As I sat next to him, I started to then open up and talk incessantly. There was so much to be said, for surely, it had been suppressed in my chest for ages. Nothing could stop me now. It was as if a dam had burst. Isn't that what a reunion is all about? Words struggled to race and catch up with the emotions, but I did not stop. It had been an absence of several decades. Why should the reunion be any less intense?

When it started to get late in the day, and I reluctantly started my long walk back to the guesthouse, I was finally at peace. The quest spread over decades of inaccessibility was triumphantly over. I had finally marked my attendance and achieved my lifelong goal. The unforgiving rays of the sun could do nothing to diminish my spirits. I had won. The marathon that I had been running for decades had come to a gratifying end with my finally overcoming the odds and returning victorious.

However, I was still crying. What kind of a meeting had this really been? Where was the father-daughter embrace? When the sun rays had poured down, why had there been no shade for me in the presence of my father? And why had my father not said a single word in all this?

Nonetheless, I was incredibly thankful to Allah Almighty. 22 May 2014 was the first day I had met my late father in my living memory, and in my few days in Aligarh, I then met him seven times altogether. Every time I went there at his grave, the tears flowed. However, the headstone was also properly washed, the grave was spruced clean and painted, and a sapling was planted on the grave. I secured a promise from the plant to not wither away but instead to bear flowers and provide shade and to take care of my father. I secured similar promises from Rafiq, the graveyard caretaker. It was not dissimilar to the way girls being married off and leaving their house beseech their younger siblings to take care of the parents.

The seven rounds of the graveyard were all I could do in those limited three days. While leaving the graveyard for the last time, I also saw a small grave marked by some grieving parents, "Let me remain anonymous, for that is my name." It painfully reminded me of my grandson's grave in Karachi whose time on Earth was merely a single day but now rests peacefully in the shade of his grandfather's grave and is marked, "Next to my grandfather, I am safe."

When I left Aligarh, I gave my silent regards to Minto-A, Minto-B, Minto-C, Minto-D hostel living residents and loud greets to the silent Minto-E residents. The graveyard had been cheekily titled Minto-E by the university students.

2

Visiting India to see my ancestral places was my foremost desire since as far back as I can remember. With my life now on its last run, I was finally in India to step in the footprints of my elders.

Chapter 2
In Ghalib's City — Delhi

There were a few hours left in my scheduled departure time from Delhi to Aligarh, the journey to the city I had awaited all my life.

Prof Irteza Karim of Delhi University had insisted that I must visit Delhi University. The university was on a term break, but professors were in attendance. I had had the pleasure of meeting Prof Irteza Karim last year at Arts Council when he had come to Karachi for the International Urdu Conference. In my meeting with him, I had presented him *Afkar-e-Hasan*, the collection of my father's writing as complied in a book format by me over fifty years after his demise. I had given it to him with the plea that if he could take it back to Aligarh in India, it would please me immensely. If the journey to Aligarh could not be made, I had pleaded that the book be added to the Delhi University library collection. He had remembered my sentimental plea and on the phone was insistent I visit Delhi University. I certainly wanted to, but I had very limited time at my disposal before my journey to Aligarh, so I promised to meet him on the way back from Aligarh.

Just the mere thought of being on the road trip of a lifetime to Aligarh, and how close to reality it was, had my heart pounding and playing with my blood pressure. To keep my excitement in check and to utilise fully the remainder of my time in Delhi, and more so to distract and keep myself engaged before the big journey, I decided to utilise the few hours at my disposal to visit the Ghalib Academy. It would be nice to visit Ballimaran, where a nomad poet, Ghalib, used to traverse the lane, composing and reciting poetry.

The cycle rickshaw in Delhi was testing my patience. It was an appalling scene, one after another, going through the back alleys of Jamia Masjid with the two-way traffic of people—beggars, labourers, artisans and the odd lot. Shops selling all kind of wares, including food, lined the narrow lanes. It was utter chaos, but people were deft and nimble in avoiding contact. In the scorching heat, the cycle rickshaws were all being pulled by frail men with rags passing for clothes on their body. They were all covered in soot and dust. Every face showed despair, suffering and helplessness but an eagerness to earn money, even if that meant this heavy and strenuous work. I was in no doubt that all these human couriers were afflicted with some life-threatening illness or the other. I thanked Allah that this menace—the insulting, dehumanising and demeaning practice of cycle rickshaw—did not exist any-

MOIST-EYED

more in Pakistan and deeply prayed that this is banned in India as well.

With this in mind, I stepped out of the cycle rickshaw midway through our journey, and while I paid for the full journey, I refused to be couriered any further. I braved the back alleys by walking until I came to a wider lane and was able to hail a taxi and get to Ballimaran Lane and reached Ghalib's house.

At the corner of the narrow Ballimaran Lane was an antiquated signpost that looked as if it might have been there since Ghalib's time. However, it did lead the way to the Ghalib house, which was the second or third house on the right side. Today, that structure is known as the Ghalib Academy.

On the stairs outside the Ghalib Academy lounged a few men, idling time. Some were sleeping, and some were chewing something. On the main door was a huge lock. This was a bit disappointing. I looked around and saw another board which stated that the visiting hours were from 11 AM to 6 PM, and Mondays was the day off. Today was not Monday, but it was 10 AM. I, however, did not have the luxury of waiting another hour.

One of my hosts accompanying me in the meantime had identified the security guard. He was one of the men on the stairs, chewing and munching. My host asked him at what time the Academy would open. "11 AM." He replied in fluent Urdu.

"Can you give us an early access?" I pleaded. "We have come from afar and we have to leave soon as well."

The security guard gave us a serious look, scrutinizing and determining that we were indeed telling the truth. He opened the lock and door for us. I tried to tip him some money, but he politely declined to accept.

As I was stepping inside the Academy, I quizzed him. "What do you know about Ghalib?"

"Well, I don't know much except that he was a big man and used to live in this place. Now, the government has taken over his place and put up his pictures all over the house inside. Now, people come from far and wide to see those pictures and the house where he lived."

I cannot think of a more underwhelming description of Ghalib, but that was the best that he could muster.

"He was a great poet of Urdu and Persian." I tried to add to his body of knowledge so that he could relay something more meaningful to future visitors. On a whim, I also asked him then, "You do know what a poet is, right?"

"The one who says poetry," he countered. "I know that. And yes, those who say great poetry are great poets."

I doubt, though, if this brief conversation increased any level of admiration in him, for Ghalib. Delhi Government, with the help of Indian Ministry of Culture, has created the Ghalib Academy and certainly given high stature and recognition to this small house in a narrow lane. I could not but praise and thank the Indian Government for this.

A few steps in, and we were inside the Ghalib Academy. On one side of the wall, his biographical details were written down for all visitors to refresh their memory, and on the other side of the wall were the biographical details of Umrao Begum. Inside on one wall was the map of the Agra house, and on another was the picture depiction of the Muradabad Haveli. Everywhere, there were Ghalib's most famous couplets adorning the walls. In one place, I saw a quote from Ralph Russel, "If Ghalib had been a poet of English language, he would have been known as the greatest poet ever." I liked the quote, although I felt that Ghalib still was the greatest poet.

At the Ghalib Academy, I also got to see the utensils from that era. I got to see the open long coat, which was the prized and most recognisable piece of clothing of Ghalib. It seemed to be in almost tatters now, and I was not even sure if it was the real one that he actually wore, but all praise for the tailor and designer for the uniqueness of that long coat. Then, there was a picture that ably depicted the after-hours preoccupation of Ghalib.

رہنے دو ابھی ساغر و مینا میرے آگے

Leave the wine glass and flagon for now, before me.

There was also a portrait of him with a pen in one hand and a hookah in another. His diwan, secured in a transparent glass case, was open on page 557, where his famous ghazal was written in his own handwriting:

یہ نہ تھی ہماری قسمت کہ وصالِ یار ہوتا

اگر اور جیتے رہتے یہی انتظار ہوتا

To have met my friend was not my fate;
A longer life would only have meant a longer wait.

It is said that some of Ghalib's favourite pastimes were flying kites and playing chausar and chess. I saw the chausar laid out as well.

On one of the posters on the wall was his couplet:

نہ ستائش کی تمنا نہ صلے کی پروا

گر نہیں ہیں مرے اشعار میں معنی نہ سہی

Not harbouring any hope for praise or compense;
If my poetry eludes you, you may dispense.

I was quite liberal in taking pictures for my digital memories. After all, my family had history that was entwined with Ghalib. When in 1862, Sir Syed Ahmed Khan visited Ghazipur, he was on the lookout for individuals who could help further his educational mission. He found many of the traits he was seeking in a certain Abdul Samad, who was the son of Molvi Muhammad Siddiq—a noble landlord of Ghazipur.

Abdul Samad was well versed in both the eastern and western subjects. His initial education had been at the German Mission High School, which is now a Government Intermediate College. Thereafter, he had moved to Allahabad, from there to Evening Christian College, and later at Allahabad University, where he had secured his law degree. He had then returned to Ghazipur, practiced law with honesty and dedication, and made a good name for himself. It was in those days that Abdul Samad had met Sir Syed, who used to be hosted at his house when Sir Syed visited Ghazipur.

It was Sir Syed's mission to introduce not just local eastern education but also western education and languages to the common masses. In 1864, he had established Queen Victoria Madrassa, about which Hali has written in *Hayat-e-Jawed* as well. When Sir Syed relocated to Aligarh, he continued to stay in touch with Abdul Samad via regular correspondence. Abdul Samad continued to fund Sir Syed's ventures from Ghazipur, and his contributions are a well-documented part of the history. Sir Syed personally invited him to be his houseguest on his next visit to Aligarh. Sir Syed also mentioned the books posted to him by Abdul Samad, including three that he authored, which are still part of the Shah Farid Alam collection in Moulana Azad Library, Aligarh.

Abdul Samad used to write excellent narratives and was a poet along with his legal skills. He had been under the mentorship of Aasi Ghazipuri.

In *Samat-al-Ikhyar*, it is mentioned that Abdul Samad used to show his drafts to Aasi Ghazipuri and got praise from him. In *Khum Khana Jawed,* Lala Siri Ram has also published some of his ghazals.

Aasi Ghazipuri also composed a lot of ghazal. Abdul Samad would most certainly have visited the same house where I now stood and would have conveyed those ghazals to Ghalib. As witnessed in *Ain al Arif*, Ghalib is said to have praised the ghazals and shown his immense pleasure that there were still people in Hindustan with such creative talent.

Abdul Samad is my great-grandfather. Molvi Abdul Samad is how he is best known. With Sir Syed and later Ghalib, his contacts are all part of history, and though buried with the passage of time, are well documented in historical records. Whenever I peek into the past, I am reminded of the great legacy of my ancestors, and I cannot but feel immense pride. Then I always ask myself:

MOIST-EYED

تھے وہ آباء تو تمہارے ہی مگر تم کیا ہو

Glory be to your forefathers indeed, but what of you?

This question always embarrasses me. We have lived our lives but maybe to live only in this generation. To remain alive in history books and to live forever in hearts and minds of people, the hoops that one needs to take, I don't know how to do so.

My father's last poetry couplet was:

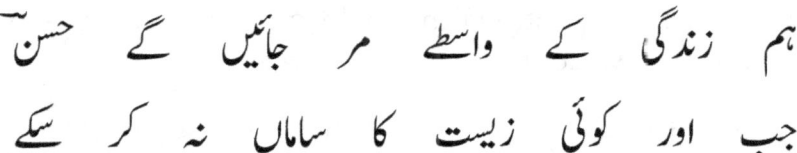

We will die at the altar of life, Hasan;
In failing to provision for our existence.

Visiting India to see my ancestral places was my foremost desire since as far back as I can remember. With my life now on its last run, I was finally in India to step in the footprints of my elders. After reinforcing my personal linkage by association with Ghalib, I was en route to Aligarh, where my father had studied, worked and died. Why he ended up becoming a steward instead of a professor is best documented in Rasheed Ahmed Siddiqui's book *Ganjaha-e-Granmaya*.

It was in this very Aligarh that my grandfather was a member of the court and secretary to Mohsin ul Mulk and Waqar ul Mulk and friends with personalities like Nawab Muzammilullah and Nawab Ishaq Khan.

It was in this very Aligarh that my great-grandfather Molvi Abdul Samad's name was carved on a gate of the illustrious university to honour him in his services for Aligarh University. It was this same Abdul Samad who refused the title of Sir out of sheer patriotism. He had stated that he does not wish to secure a title from the British Government, which would grant him a piece of land of his own country as part of the deal.

I was en route to the city that unquestionably was the beneficiary of immense contributions of at least three generations of my family.

3

The sun was bearing down on me at 48°C or 49°C, but while aware of the heat, I was oblivious to the inconvenience. The burning desire of my heart was infinitely greater than the sun's rays. I felt such contentment in my heart that I did not have words to express my joy, and thus, maybe only I was aware of being in paradise.

Chapter 3

Aligarh — Two and a Half Days

The unbelievable was finally in motion. I was en route to Aligarh from Delhi. My heart and mind were matching the speed of the car, if not more.

I had been only about two years old when I had been orphaned from my Aligarh land. At two, I could have hardly left any footprints that I could go back and retrace, so this was more about retracing my family and elder's footprints than mine, accompanied with a baggage of more than half a century of yearning.

There were almost no memories, so hardly any chance of rekindling any. I was essentially in quest of finding stories that pertained to my father and grandparents. They had lived honest, hardworking, dedicated and meaningful lives, and I was curious to see if that had led to any impact or legacy that had withstood the test of time. I knew their names and deeds had survived their mortal life, but I wanted to see that impact and legacy for myself.

Even centuries cannot erase the exceptional good work of honest minds and souls. Take for example the work of the godfather of Aligarh—Sir Syed Ahmed Khan. Can any coming century repay the debt and magnitude of his impact or ignore his contributions?

Most certainly, the contributions of my father and grandfather pale in comparison to that of Sir Syed. However, they were certainly intertwined with Sir Syed's time and efforts. I wondered if my elders' contribution was somehow, somewhat acknowledged and remembered as well.

I was racing towards Aligarh to seek answer to that question. I was quite hopeful that I would be able to unearth their footprints because I was determined to do so. I knew I would find them in some street or lane of Aligarh or some room in some house, in some corner of a library or a mosque, and if nowhere else, then in someone's heart or mind. It was a journey that I had undertaken way too late, but better late than never.

The car journey from Delhi to Aligarh was a mixed bag. Sometimes for a certain stretch, it was smooth, and at other times, torrid. Initially, the road was paved, but as Aligarh came nearer, the journey became rough. It is an absolute shame that despite being a very heavy commute between Delhi and Aligarh, the Indian Government has not invested in even the very basic carpeting and maintenance of this road. There were evident neglects that one could see and feel on the road journey. I have asked this same question on many roads of my own country, and today I was asking the same questions in a foreign land as well.

All through the journey, despite the mind being in overdrive, I was trying to take mental snapshots of the route. Long bland roads, vulnerable mud houses, trees of all shapes and sizes, small villages, kids on the street. They might not mean much as my quest was ahead of me, but still, I was not able to ignore all this scenery as it whizzed past.

I got a bit emotional wondering how many times my father and grandfather would have travelled on similar (or worse?) roads. En route, I also saw the Aligarh exhibition ground, and a few stories about the place I had heard from others came to mind. However, soon, the journey culminated, with us entering the hallowed perimeter of the Aligarh Muslim University that I had always dreamt of stepping back into. I was finally back at the campus where I had spent my early days of my long-lost childhood.

Prof Saghir Afraheim of Urdu department called as soon as I was at the hostel. "We are waiting for you." I too had waited an eternity for this.

In the car that he sent to the hostel, I was transported promptly to the Urdu department. I was ecstatic beyond words. I was truly over the moon. Today was the culmination of decades of yearning. I was now in the venerated department of Prof Rasheed Ahmed Siddiqui, where my father would have spent many great hours with his professor and mentor. Somehow, I felt the freshness of those bygone moments. While physically, my father and Rasheed sahab were not there, I could feel their fragrance. At this time, I also remembered Prof Ahsaan Rasheed. He was my professor at Karachi University, and once after graduating, I had told him, "Your father was my father's teacher, and you are my teacher. But from today, my family gets to join the noble profession, as I have become a professor." He had given a great smile on my comment. A great smile indeed.

In front of me, on the wall, amongst others was the picture of Rasheed sahab. My eyes were looking at the picture with immense respect. I did not know if this room was the same room where Rasheed sahab and my father would have sat together. Lest it not be the case, I did not inquire.

The president of Urdu department was Prof Aqil Ahmed Siddiqui. He accorded me great respect, and I was feeling blessed knowing that he was bringing dignity to the chair that once had been graced by one of his most illustrious predecessors, Rasheed sahab. Other professors who had gathered in the room included previous past president of the Urdu department Prof Muhammad Zahid, Prof Jamal Hussain, Prof Tariq Chattari, Dr Seema Sagheer, Dr Qamar Ul Huda Faridi, Research scholar Muhammad Furqan Sanbhali, Muhammad Salman Muhammad Shahid, Ikram Waris, Abdul Rehman, Muhammad Maroof, Zameerullah, Kaif Farshori, Muhammad Farhan, Neha Iqbal, and Fouzia. Saghir sahab introduced me with great eloquence, but what was mesmerizing for me was repeatedly hearing my father's name in this gathering and sur-

MOIST-EYED

rounding. This was the tonic for my soul and music to my ears. Why else had I come here if not for this?

Prof Qazi Afzal stepped out of the room when I mentioned Aal Ahmed Saroor in my talk. I thought maybe the session had run too long and he had other errands to cater to, but he shortly returned with an autobiography of Aal sahab titled *Dreams Remain*. He signed it in my name and gave it to me, for which I didn't have words to thank him.

Autobiographies are at times written in that last part of one's age, when history may get a bit mixed up and some dates and events are incorrectly remembered. With Aal sahab, it was the same. He mentioned the age at death of my father as fifty, although my father passed away at the young age of forty. If only he had another ten years, I would most certainly have memories of my father. I would have cultivated more memories and remembered his form, his breath, his fragrance.

Prof Saghir took me on a tour of the department and also showed me many of the books published by the department. He was kind enough to give me many of those books as well. In that meeting, I also got a chance to narrate an article that I had written on my father, delivered in a free flow of tears, which received standing ovation.

I was flying high in the clouds. I was finally feeling blessed that my destiny had eventually brought me to the alma mater where my father graduated as a student and had wished to become a professor. His professor

Rasheed Ahmad Siddiqui had different ideas, though. He had said, "It was difficult to counter argue to the rationale of the university officials that if not today, then tomorrow or later, a professor in Urdu can be found, but to find an honest steward like Hasan Abdullah is impossible."

I used the opportunity to place *Afkar-e-Hasan* in the department. This was a compilation of my father's writings that I had been able to scrape together from varied sources over the decades and probably the only thing I had ever done for him in my life. I was probably unable to communicate the extent of my profound gratitude to Prof Saghir, but I am hopeful he understood the depths of my gratefulness.

My heart was in eternal bliss being feted at a university where I had not studied a single day, all thanks to the legacy of my father and grandfather.

I also got a chance to see the office of *Thezeeb-ul-Ikhlaq*. Prof Saghir had recently become editor of the landmark magazine, which has a well-documented and illustrious history.

It was heartening to see how smoothly things were progressing. In that beautiful office, I met some great personalities. In their talk, I could see the entire culture and tradition of Aligarh. There, I became a life member of Sir Syed's *Thezeeb-ul-Ikhalq* journal. I was offered many of the past issues. Conscious of the airline luggage and weight restriction, I had to be very choosy in which ones I packed, although the desire was to take them all.

MOIST-EYED

Almost all the professors I met complained that the number of days I had allocated to Aligarh were insufficient and that I should have come when the campus was buzzing with activity, but I was truly grateful for whatever limited time I had at my disposal. Even seconds are worth a lot when you have waited for your chance to visit for more than half a century.

Prof Saghir went overboard with his hospitality. With him, I also got to visit Habib Manzil, which was the present abode of Riaz Ur Rehman Sherwani. Riaz sahab's great-grandfather was Habib Ur Rehman Sherwani, who had a very prominent role in Aligarh at that time. His record and services to the Aligarh Muslim University is well known and second to none. For me, this connection was important, as my grandfather had worked for many years with him together, and on the death of my father, he had personally visited from Delhi to Aligarh to pay his respects. The meeting in Habib Manzil was thus a meeting of a grandson and a granddaughter. Two families, two generations later were meeting for the first time. Riaz Ur Rehman sahab was indeed a living testament to the greatness of his predecessors and here I was sitting and thinking:

Glory be to your forefathers indeed, but what of you?

Riaz Ur Rehman Sherwani sahab's conversational pureness, richness and delicate personality had me captivated. While there was tea and biscuits in front of me, his conversation was really all I needed to enrich my soul. When he signed his copy of book *Dhoop Chaoun* and presented it to me, I could not but admire my luck. History had finally raced ahead and caught up with the present. It was these moments that I had craved for, for so many decades.

I wondered how many times my father and grandfather would have entered this very Habib Mazil. And today, here I was, sitting in that very house. Maybe this was the first of our many meetings, or the first and last one, given the cross-border mistrust challenges that impede travel. Nonetheless, this meeting was something that had made my life meaningful in many ways. Again, I stood indebted to Prof Saghir for this.

Then came the second day, which was reserved for Hakim Zil-e-Rehman. He was indeed the Indian version of our Pakistani Lutfullah Khan. Lutfullah sahab had created a world out of preserving voices of the legends in Pakistan, as a unique hobby of his. I have written an entire article on him, and the passing reference here does him no justice.

Hakim Zil-e-Rehman sahab was the proud owner of the Ibn-e-Sina Academy. The Academy was nothing short of an ocean of amazement. I witnessed the entire culture and history of the India there. Thousands of years old artefacts, books, and pictures were neatly displayed. Just to see each with proper interest and dedication would require several days. This was not possible in a short cursory visit.

At 74 years of age, Hakim Zil-e-Rehman sahab is a giant amongst us mere mortals with a long list of incredible achievements. He has authored over forty books and been awarded countless times. He is an expert in organic medicine and, over the decades, has set up several institutions. The library he had created was populated with Arabic, Persian, Urdu, Sanskrit, and English books. In his lifetime, he had been on the editorial board of multiple journals and clearly accomplished more than what people can even dream over multiple lifetimes. Compared to how people like Hakim Zil-e-Rehman sahab make every second worthwhile, we are certainly guilty of wasting away our day and nights. May Allah bless him with more productive and prosperous years of health and energy so that he can still accomplish more—which will be truly beneficial for the coming generations.

I was truly blessed to have met him and other luminaries of Aligarh. My last day in Aligarh was scheduled for a visit to Moulana Azad Library, where Dr Amjad hosted a fantastic reception. I was delighted because my books ***Afkar-e-Hasan***, ***Kalaam-e-Ashraf***, and ***Kamal-e-Hasan*** were gratefully received and logged in the library, which house publications of great authors from around the world.

In this library, there were also the written manuscripts and personal collection of books of my great-grandfather

Molvi Abdul Samad. They were there on the shelf in the library as part of Shah Farid Alam collection. Dr Amjad was extremely hospitable and gave a lot of his valuable time as he took me on a tour of the library. We had a lot of photographs taken along with generous supply of tea.

At the library, I also saw the Aligarh Institute Gazette Section where all the bound magazines were placed neatly. I also saw the All India Muslim Educational Conference Aligarh weekly newspaper *Conference Gazette*, in which at #47 binding I found the article written by Rasheed Ahmed Siddiqui regarding my father, which he later compiled in his landmark book *Ganjaha-e-Granmaya*.

I told Dr Amjad that I have written manuscripts from my grandfather and other university trustees dating almost 150 years back. The papers are parched, and the ink is fading away fast. He promised to take good care of them if I could somehow find a way to bring them over. I hope to do so.

From the library, Prof Saghir continued to show me around, and we also went to Sir Syed House. The visionary, creator and benefactor of Aligarh, Sir Syed Ahmed Khan would be truly pleased even to this date to know that students are still benefitting from the institution he set up so long ago.

This cloud has always rained, this cloud will always rain.

MOIST-EYED

In Sir Syed House, there was Sir Syed everywhere. Things relating to him—items, furniture, clothing, writings—seem preserved for posterity. I took a lot of photographs there, including those of his signature and of the showcases displaying his possessions.

The in-charge of Sir Syed House was able to quickly retrieve a writing of Sir Syed Ahmed Khan relating to my great-grandfather. I was absolutely over the moon to realise that Sir Syed House housed a piece of history that related to my own elders. I was incredibly proud and happy.

During my days in Aligarh, from morning to evening, I continued to walk from one part of the campus to the other. The sun was bearing down on me at 48°C or 49°C, but while aware of the heat, I was oblivious to the inconvenience. The burning desire of my heart was infinitely greater than the sun's rays. I felt such contentment in my heart that I did not have words to express my joy, and thus, maybe only I was aware of being in paradise. Not a second went by when I did not thank Allah for this blessing. My family tree is littered with diamonds, and I was reaping praise and respect for their works of distant past.

Leaving Sir Syed House, I was still thinking of that verse:

Glory be to your forefathers indeed, but what of you?

The night that I had to leave Aligarh, I became concerned and agitated. I did not want the day to end. Every passing second brought me closer to my departure. I was packing up my luggage, and all that was going through my mind was the action replay of the past few days from the departments to the libraries to the graveyard and the lovely people I had met and the stories I had heard.

I was still deep in reliving my time spent in Aligarh when Prof Saghir brought in Mehr Elahi Nadeem. Prof Saghir had two newspaper clippings in his hand. The first was from *Inquilab*, and the second one from *Sahara*, and it had pictures of my outings and activities in Aligarh from the previous day. And after that, whichever place I went, the news of my arrival had already arrived in advance through those news items.

Mehr Ali sahab had brought with him a few writings of my grandfather. I asked in astonishment as to where did he get those.

"I am working on these," was his answer.

"What kind of work?" I asked in continued amazement.

He mentioned that he was doing a biography on Nawab Muzammilullah on the request of Nawab's nephew and nieces. "These are some letters that Abul Hasan, your grandfather, had written to him."

These were truly historic letters, and the university takes pride in having them in its collection. I had no idea about these letters, which had been found in Nawab Muzammilullah's library collection.

He mentioned that he had been in *Thezeeb-ul-Ikhlaq's* office earlier, listening to my talk about my father and had realised I was Molvi Abul Hasan's granddaughter. "I thus came to show you these writings."

Left speechless, I was looking at him with aghast appreciation and gratitude. There are still people out there in the world who are selflessly working to keep the past alive. I was already indebted to him for life.

He then took out a postcard. I looked at it from afar and quizzed with a chuckle if they still used postcards. He patiently insisted in a somewhat hushed tone that I give it a closer read. As soon as I saw the first line, which was the date, I shrieked. "It's the date that my father died."

"Keep reading," he politely insisted.

The writing was of Nawab Muqtada Khan Sherwani, who had sent this postcard to Nawab Habibur Rehman Sherwani, stating that the Steward of Aligarh Muslim University, Hasan Abdullah, had passed away earlier that day. Six decades later, I was holding a postcard announcing the death of my father. It had been written when I was barely two years old and unable to read or write or remember almost anything from that time. Hasan Abdullah is peacefully buried in Minto-E graveyard, and here I was holding a postcard from that era, six decades later, and reading it. The postcard is the property of Mehr Elahi Nadeem.

In Aligarh, every place was a Yaadoun ki Baraat. They marked the battlefield where my father has succumbed. However, today, ironically, this procession of memories was giving me a new lease of life of my own.

It seemed that my father had plans in the works to provide a stable life for us. However, he had been betrayed by life's fickleness, leaving his family stranded at an uncertain stage where we did not know the meaning or joy of life and what his death entailed. The question remained: who was going to lead us down this journey of understanding?

While bidding farewell to Aligarh, I was unsure if I would ever have the fortune of reliving it again.

4

Till then, I had always seen Taj Mahal in print or pictures, but today, it shone in front of my eyes in its rightful glory. On the corner of Jumna River, the Taj Mahal is truly a sight to behold, and I felt glad to have been there, just like the other countless millions who come to see it for real.

Chapter 4

Two Colleges in Agra and the Taj Mahal

My journey to India was driven largely by the quest to trace my father's footsteps and our lost heritage. I wanted to visit every place he might have frequented and see if those places remembered him as well. Following Aligarh, my next stop was Agra, and the date with destiny had been preordained for 24 May 2014.

Agra was once known as Akbarabad and the capital of undivided India. It boasts one of the modern wonders of the world, the Taj Mahal, which with its rich history has served as a symbol of architectural beauty and love and a magnet for tourists. The craftsman had to embrace the painful reality of having their hands chopped as an eternal promise never to recreate their marvel anywhere else. Centuries later, their sacrifice endured. Visitors seek to try and understand the love and despair that was behind this marvel, and that has remained its enduring appeal.

When Sikandar Khan Lodhi, the most successful ruler of the Lodhi dynasty and an accomplished Persian poet, was setting up the Agra city on the sides of River Jumna, little did he know that this place would one day be known around the world for its architectural marvel.

Could Mumtaz Mahal, Queen Arjumand Bano Begum, have ever imagined such a beautiful final resting place for herself, despite requesting one? Her Mughal emperor husband Shah Jahan certainly delivered on that, not that it was quid pro quo for the fourteen children she delivered for him. While he was rich enough to have laden the tomb with gold, the Taj, with its architectural perfection and monumental beauty, serves infinitely more as evidence of his undying love and devotion for her.

As ably quipped by the poet Sahir Ludhianvi:

اِک شہنشاہ نے دولت کا سہارا لے کر
ہم غریبوں کی محبت کا اُڑایا ہے مذاق

With the emperor flaunting his fortune;
We, the broke, had our affections mocked.

Whereas the poet Shakeel Badayuni stated:

MOIST-EYED

اِک شہنشاہ نے بنوا کے حسیں تاج محل
ساری دُنیا کو محبت کی نشانی دی ہے

With the emperor building the majestic Taj Mahal;
The world has been bestowed the testimonial of love.

Taj Mahal is probably the top reason tourists today, come to Agra. I had it number two on my list.

My primary reason was to go visit those educational institutions of Agra which for centuries have been spreading the gift of knowledge and from which my father had likewise benefited.

I spent forty years associated with the noble profession of imparting education. I know very well that in every student, there is a meaningful presence of gratitude for at least one educational institution, which is usually where they studied and spent the prime of their youth. That period is the most nostalgic and treasured by any student.

It is often only within the corridors, classrooms and campus setting at an educational institute that one can truly start curating the purpose of one's life. It is also where an opportunity is accorded to impart the lessons of life to others. With the blue pen marking yes or success and a red pen marking a no or fail; one can convey the essentials and impart the dos and don'ts of life. How to think and what not to think? How to live and how not to live? These guidelines can be the blueprint for the rest of one's life.

Hence, the time spent at educational institutions remains the most meaningful and pleasant phase of any person's life. I have cultivated a deep appreciation for my educational institutions. I have learned from these education institutions and strive to mentor others with affirmative strokes of the blue pen.

For my father, two educational institutions in Agra would have held immense value—one where he studied and the other where he taught.

Setting out from Aligarh, my journey was dedicated to finding those two institutions.

With the car on the way, my mind went out on a journey of its own. The tall trees, swishing wind, alternating narrow and wide streets, road corners were all part of that mind journey and conversation. At one point in time, the car came to a sudden halt at a roundabout corner. There were a couple of street vendors on the side selling sliced cucumbers. With a bit of spice sprinkled over them and all the skin, they were packed and handed to me in the car in a plastic. A familiar sight in Delhi and Aligarh, I had now encountered this in Agra as well.

My apparently out of town driver struggled to find St John's College and stopped several times to ask for directions. Indifferent or unaware, people just walked past. I saw a few young men coming through. I thought they might know. I called out to them and asked the route to St John's College. They pointed us in the general but right direction, and we continued. Until we had the youth give us the steer, who I thought would be best suited to know where the college was, we seemed to have been going in circles. Thankfully, the youth still know the way to the college. We got to another bend in the road and then onto a main road, and on the left, we found the old, solid building of St John's College.

It was summer break. The campus looked deserted. A few students were loitering around, probably to take some exam shortly. The car was driven inside.

Despite being early morning, the sun was spitting fire. I, however, almost shivered realising that I could probably be standing at the very place where my father might have stood decades back.

After taking a few steps, I got to a courtyard. On the notice board were roll numbers and classroom numbers. After having done this for over forty years, it was still nice to see something familiar. The exam season is the same everywhere. In front of me was a room where there were a few professors going about. As I neared, I saw pile of exam scripts and a duty chart where they were trying to determine which room was their exam duty.

I knew this was considered as a restricted area during exam time and thus stood outside the room and requested a female teacher to come out. She did, and I spoke with her. I told her, "After 1927, I have only now been able to return, and I would like to meet the principal."

I think there was something in my face or my voice, but despite my strange comment, the Christian professor proved quite welcoming. She invited me into the room and got me a cold drink. In the meantime, the bell rang, and the exam started. I waited until the principal arrived, and I was shown into his room. While walking in, I felt like a student with trepidation entering the principal's office. This was the college where my father had graduated from. The principal was looking at me. I am sure he was curious to know who I was and what I wanted. He had gotten up to welcome me.

I said that I was visiting from Pakistan and would appreciate if he had a few minutes to spare. In fluent Urdu, he welcomed me and offered me a chair. Without even knowing my name, his welcome on the basis of the name of merely my country was very reassuring and welcoming for me. It felt really good.

As I sat down, I told him that my late father had done his BS from St John's College in 1927 and briefly taught here as well. "I have come to India and here for the first time to relive those times." He was listening to me with rapt attention, despite it sounding quite weird that I had made the journey just to see a college where my father had studied almost a century back.

MOIST-EYED

I told him that I do not know in which class he used to sit and which staff room he would have occupied with other colleagues. I was aware that a lot of construction would have erased even the remnants from those times. He said there are still some rooms from those times but in very bad shape. He took me on a tour of the college. Room Number 8 had a story of its own. I sat on a bench and put my hand on the desk. Maybe he had sat on this bench. Maybe on another bench that I just saw. I looked at each and every bench in the room. The blackboard on the wall had sunk deep in the wall. Hundreds of professors over the decades would have written in chalk on that very board, and many a subjects, sketches and facts would have been conveyed to thousands of students. I put my head on the bench, and my tears puddled the decaying wooden bench. This was one way to carve my "I was here" onto the wooden desk.

I silently addressed my father and said, "Baba, I have come here while retracing your life and felt I saw you as a young student."

The campus was a blend of the old and new. It had moved forward and yet was stuck, in some aspects, in the past, and in so many good ways.

We retired back to the principal's room. The principal of St John's College was Prof Alexander Lall. He had done his MSc and PhD from Agra, along with a few other qualifications from Germany.

Here I was, at the college that my father had left 87 years ago. Prof Lall continued to hear me out with rapt attention.

He said that he was extremely impressed with my quest and delighted that I was back in the college to retrace some of those memories of my father. He said that he could understand my emotions. He wished he had ready access to old records but promised to unearth some from that time, if he could. He made frequent mentions that he was extremely happy to have met me. The feelings were indeed mutual.

I requested a favour from him by stating that it was my wish that my father's book that I had compiled finds a permanent place in the college library. He said that only a handful of teachers and students in the college read the Urdu script, but he would nonetheless be honoured to have the book placed in the library and did so immediately. I could not thank him enough for his kind gesture.

St John's College was built in 1850 and was now into its second century. Of the thousands of its graduates, one had been my father as well. I felt proud with such association.

Professor Lall was exemplary in his hospitality. He also gave me a letter, the contents of which mean a lot to me.

I told him that in St John's College, historically there was a tradition of Mushaira. While today, the Department of Urdu or Persian does not exist at the college, but back in the days, those departments were the crown jewels of the college. And it was during that period, while being a professor for a short while at St John's College, on 15 January 1941, my father had participated in the Anjuman Taraqqi Urdu Annual Mushaira and read a poem. That poem is part of the book **Afkar-e-Hasan**.

This historical information delighted Professor Lall immensely, and he promised that in a future programme at the college campus, he would really like to invite me as a special guest. Overwhelmed with emotions, it took me a while to compose words of gratitude. His verbal gesture was a significant honour for me indeed.

As I took leave and said goodbye to the principal, it seemed the entire campus was also murmuring a farewell to me.

The next stop was Agra College. I had already asked Professor Lall for directions to this college. This was the college where my father had taught for a considerable time. Going into this very college, I was again very emotional. A teacher welcomed me and informed me that the principal was away for a meeting but would come in due course. In the meantime, I was invited to take a tour of the college.

Exams were being conducted in this college as well and thus kept the staff occupied. I met many professors. All welcomed me with open arms and were delighted to learn of my background. There was a lone Muslim young professor. Her name was Shadaan, and she was from Lucknow and taught English at the college. She was delighted to have met for the first time any professor from Pakistan. She invited me to a meal at her home and complained on my trip being too short. The hospitality I received everywhere was overwhelming. I promised that if I had another chance in life to come back to Agra, I would take up on her offer for a meal.

Seeing the Agra College classroom, staff room, library and labs, I was overcome with similar feelings that I had earlier in the day when I was at St John's College. These buildings and institutions had withstood the tests of time, but the people of that era were long gone for the eternal abode, with my father having left in an even greater hurry. Even in Agra College, Urdu and Persian departments were no longer functional. Apparently, the last professor had gotten his transfer posting to Lucknow. I found this quite sad, because this is the same Agra where Ghalib used to live, where awesome mushairas were a norm rather than an exception and where in many such gatherings my father had recited his kalaam as well.

Anjuman Taraqqi Urdu had held a Mushaira on 9 September 1926. This would have been the time when my father would still have been a student. Here, he had recited one of his ghazal.

On 19 December 1936, the 9th Annual All India Mushaira had been staged at Agra College. Here too, my father had participated with his ghazal. On 23 May 1938,

MOIST-EYED

Agra College had held another Mushaira. My father had recited his ghazal.

In Bazme-Iqbal, a Mushaira was held on 21 September 1940, where he recited his kalaam. A couplet from it is as follows:

نظر سے دُور سہی دل میں تم کو پاتا ہوں
شبِ درازِ جدائی بھی اب دراز نہیں

Not in sight, but you are certainly cherished in my heart;
Even the long night of separation is no longer endless.

The Grand All India Mushaira organised by Seemab Literary Academy was held in Agra on 30 November 1940. A couplet from it is as follows:

بار امانتِ عظیم تُو نے اُٹھا لیا تھا کیوں
حوصلہ اب وہ کیا ہوا تاب و تواں کہاں گئی

Why did you take on the burdensome responsibility of safe keeping;
Where has your courage departed,
what of energy and vibrancy?

In December 1940, a Mushaira was held at Victoria High School, Agra, in which my father had also participated. A couplet from then is as follows:

میرے خدا یہ بے کسی کس سے کہوں میں حالِ دل
ہنس کے وہ شوخ یوں کہے تیرے خدا کو کیا ہوا

Dear God, who do I converse with about my glum situation? For they playfully belittle, questioning, "wither your God?."

Agra is also the city from where he caught the illness that led to his sudden demise in Aligarh.

He had gone to Agra for some work. A few friends had set up an event in his honour. He was not feeling well, and his friends suggested he make a short speech and excuse himself. However, given the elaborate arrangements that had been done for the event, he stood and spoke for two and a half hours. This exacerbated his illness. He was brought to Aligarh but, after a few days' illness, lost the battle of life. Sitting in Agra College, I was going over this timeline, as detailed in Prof Rasheed Ahmed Siddiqui's essay about my father.

Principal Dr M K Rawat had arrived by then. He apologised for my having to wait and welcomed me with genuine hospitality. Initially, he had assumed I was some col-

MOIST-EYED

lege professor from Pakistan who was perchance in the area and had stumbled onto the college.

I detailed my reason for being there. I presented to him **Afkar-e-Hasan** and, on page 296 of the book, showed him the Agra College principal's glowing character certificate, given on 2 May 1941, in my father's name.

Principal Rawat's hospitality was truly memorable, and he also wrote me a beautiful letter. We clicked many photographs, and he was delighted to receive the book **Afkar-e-Hasan** as well to be placed in the college library. He wished that our paths cross again, both in India and Pakistan. What could be more wonderful sentiments than that for me?

The college founded in 1821 is now 193 years old. They are aiming to do their 200 years' celebration. If I live that long, an invitation will come my way, and if I can make that journey, I will do so with pleasure.

On leaving the college, I had one last look behind and remembered my father's last couplet.

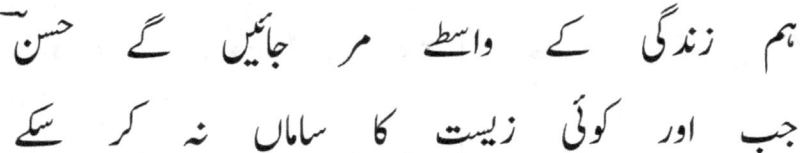

We will die at the altar of life, Hasan,
In failing to provision for our existence.

In all likelihood, this was his last couplet, which was written in Agra itself, as after returning from Agra, he died in fifteen days' time. This couplet, dated 30 August 1946, was the last note in his diary.

While leaving the college, I was feeling incredibly down in so many ways, but it also came with a towering sense of gratitude that I had had an opportunity to step into the shoes of my father and retrace his journey. With the opportunity accorded to leave behind his book at both the colleges, I felt I had left behind something for posterity. After all, what more could an orphaned daughter with no memory of him do half a century later.

The only other thing left to do in Agra was to visit Taj Mahal and praise Shah Jahan, which literally means King of the World. Agra is full of historical places, and one day in the city is clearly not enough. However, since in fifteen days, I had to travel over five cities in India, these were the only few hours I could apportion to Agra.

Till then, I had always seen Taj Mahal in print or pictures, but today, it shone in front of my eyes in its rightful glory. On the corner of Jumna River, the Taj Mahal is truly a sight to behold, and I felt glad to have been there, just like the other countless millions who come to see it for real.

On my return from Agra, I was thinking that one such evening a long time ago, my father too had bid adieu to this city. That had proven to be his last journey before the inevitable journey to his last abode in the Aligarh grave-

MOIST-EYED

yard, without any chance to think as to how his wife and young children would survive without him.

That task fell on the shoulders of his young, widowed wife to figure out.

5

However, no expert has been able to look at the skeleton and tell the name of that person, how he lived his life, what gave him pleasure and sadness, and how many tales of happiness or despair that skeleton had braved. His thoughts are lost forever.

Chapter 5

Train Journey — Aligarh to Azamgarh

The return from Agra was very late into the night, but I was now back at the Aligarh Hostel 1, Room 7.

The last few days' engagements were still creating a buzz in my mind. I was going to live and relieve these moments for the rest of my life. When I had entered this city, it had unleashed a torrent of emotions in me. I had last left this city at the age of two. Maybe some vague memories of those two years might still be residing in some deep recesses of the mind, but they are like the ancient writing, which would need an expert to decipher. I am yet to find an expert who could unearth and recreate those memories, if any, into vivid moving images for me. The next best alternative was to preserve in my mind all that I experienced on this trip.

When they dig out old coins, archaeologists can work out and identify the period they belong to. When a skeleton is unearthed, they can tell from how long ago it was. Mohenjo-Daro is unearthed and recognised as one of the earliest civilizations on planet Earth. However, no expert has been able to look at the skeleton and tell the name of that person, how he lived his life, what gave him pleasure and sadness, and how many tales of happiness or despair that skeleton had braved. His thoughts are lost forever. His family links—father, mother, siblings—cannot be unearthed and reunited, and neither can we tell how long he lived and with whom. What were his successes and failures in life? When deceased, one cannot dictate the well-being of the survivors. Mankind has some knowledge, but not all. Allama Iqbal had said:

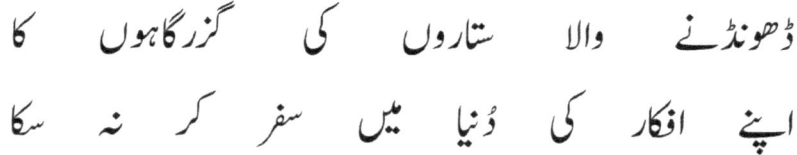

The one who pursued the orbits of the stars;
Failed to navigate the realm of his thoughts.

The realm of thoughts is quite cruel. It clings to life like a termite and one can never get rid itself of it. I tried desperately to recollect my life's first two years of Aligarh in my three days there but without any success. Of those times, what I could barely remember was the fleeting feeling of some hand that would guide me as I took my first steps. He would never let me fall and taught me how to walk. That hand would have been of my father. And when I used to get tired, I found comfort and solace in his lap.

MOIST-EYED

In my three days in Aligarh, I very much tried to see if I could recollect more from that time but failed. I tried to jog my memory to remember his face but couldn't. And then, it was time to leave. I had endeavoured to save as much of this city in my eyes and my mind as I could. The heat of this city had failed to dampen my spirits. Even the rustling of the leaves in the trees was a sound I captured in my memory.

The empty campus, deserted roads, girls driving scooters, a few students scurrying around with books in their hand, small cars laden with files and books in the back seat were all memories that I was accumulating to relish not just now but also into the future. I had been dreaming of seeing this place for six decades and now I had been here, and it was time to leave.

The books that I had brought with me to distribute had dwindled to almost none. I had chanced excess luggage weight at my flight to bring those books here. I was still in disbelief that my father's books were now in India, in those illustrious libraries of illustrious colleges and universities that he had frequented almost a century earlier. This was my life's most crowning achievement. It was so because I owed this to my father and now felt the debt had been somewhat repaid. The relief can only be sensed by someone who had thought of such a debt and then worked hard to repay it.

I was truly grateful to the Aligarh Muslim University graveyard that had given some of its space to my father.

The grave had seemed to complain to me for not having come before or often. The occupant of that grave had left behind five children, and none had ever been able to come to say fateha at his grave. Ofcourse the grave dweller did not know that India had been partitioned a year after his demise and that Pakistan had been born, and we had relinquished all. People had been displaced and borders, and rules of passport and visa had created an impregnable wall. The border tensions built over the decades thereafter did nothing to ease the mobility.

I had felt that the grave was complaining. I had stood next to the black gate and poured my heart out in the graveyard. I had felt a response that assured me that he now understood my tardiness and prior absence. Sometimes, the desire is there, and so are the resources to make them happen, but still, things go awry. I tried to reply that I have prayed fateha at the side of my father's grave not just in dreams but in my waking hours as well.

In those three days in Aligarh, I completed seven trips to my father's grave. An odyssey, a pilgrimage in so many ways.

My next stop was Ghazipur. This was the city in which I came into this world.

I used to have a mini globe on my principal's desk at the college in Karachi, where I worked for over forty years. I had often turned it around, trying to spin it to see the world. Even when I was small, playing with the globe

MOIST-EYED

was one of my favourite pastimes. Every book of geography starts with a world map and ends with a world map. Deserts are brown, and seas are blue. Cities are marked as dots. In our school exams, we used to have to make country maps and name them. We also had to point out the location of the city that the examiner was looking for. I used to mark those cities Ghazipur but always made sure before submitting the answer script to erase that and put in the right city name. However, the first name I used to label any city would be Ghazipur. I guess I wanted to dupe myself into thinking that regardless of how huge the world maybe, my world was just Ghazipur.

Ghazipur is a city with a very familiar tale to that of which is said of the province of Sindh and Raja Dahir. An elderly woman of Ghazipur, to save her young daughter from the cruel ruler of that place, had pleaded with the king of those time. In those days, apparently, the king had time to listen to the travails of their populace and actually act upon them as well, quite unlike the present, where campaign promises die at the campaign trail as soon as the victory is assured. Justice at the doorstep is an alien concept for rulers of now. This old woman's plea reached a just king of those times, and his name was Feroz Shah Tuglaq. The Delhi King then sent a small army unit under the able command of Ameer Masood to go and battle out the unjust rule of Raja Manda Tachkoni.

Similar to Muhammad Bin Qasim, Ameer Masood reached this fertile Southern Hindustan land and, after a valiant battle, defeated the cruel ruler and got relief for the old woman. King Feroz Shah, delighted with the outcome, gave him the title of Malik Al Saadat Ghazi.

Ameer Masood in 730H (i.e., Year 1330), then founded a city which today is known as Ghazipur. Ameer Masood proved to be a just and able ruler of his time. He lived for some 33 years in this city, and in his tenure, the city became the hub of culture, education and religious and political activity and in his times was known as one of the wealthiest places.

And in this very city, a few hundred years later, a house was built at the corner of Bednath roundabout. This house was called Hasan Manzil. And in this house, in a room with six doors, in a corner bed, I was born. This is where I first breathed and my arrival was announced. It was here for the first time my father would have picked me up and kissed me and my grandfather would have said the call to prayers in my ears. The first of most things in my life started in this Hasan Manzil, whose inheritor I am today. However, with mass migration, inheritances don't really survive, and I was robbed of this with my dislocation.

Now six decades late, I was en route back to my birthplace on the Kaifi train from Aligarh to Ghazipur. This train had been dedicated by the Muslim film actor of India, Shabana Azmi, to the memory of her father, Kaif Azmi. I like this a lot, as I too was a lost daughter on a journey to find my father. Once on the Kaifi train, I started

MOIST-EYED

looking out of the window, and my mind started running at a speed faster than the train.

I was back on a train, after a gap of almost forty years. In my student days, I had done many rail journeys, but those were different times. People were trustworthy, and I had travelled from Karachi to up north all alone without any fear or concerns. My mother used to pack me meals. She was worried about my hunger on the journey but not worried about my safety. Those were the days when as a student, there weren't the kinds of threats that exist today. Elders on the journey readily took the younger ones in their protection by terming them their daughters, and we used to reach our destination unharmed.

Before sitting in trains, I always used to make a quick detour to the bookstall of the train station to buy the train timetable and some other books, despite bringing some magazines from home. Without reading, the journey never seemed pleasant, or even complete. The window seat was always my favourite regardless of the cabin class. The romance of the night journey was a pleasure in itself. It was also quite necessary to peep out of the window to see the name of the train station, and I used to check against the timetable to see if the arrival was on time or late for that station.

In those days, the trains did not used to run hours or days late. All stations were normally of the same type with the same kind of noise. In warmer months, it was about cold drinks, and in cold months, it was about warm boiled eggs. Bread and pakoras were aplenty. While journeying through barren lands and deep jungles, the peculiar noise of the train engine and whistle was better than most music. In every train journey, I used to be reminded of Josh Malihabad's nazm titled "Train Journey", and I used to marvel at his writing.

What happened next, though, was that we grew old, and the world changed. The coin in the book became a lot of change in the purse, and we moved on to air travel, where before departure, an airhostess advises us to wear our seat belts and in monotones advises us of the expected altitude and flight time and weather on arrival. If you ask me, there is nothing that can rival the joy of a train journey. But I do concede that the world has changed, and gone are the days of my summer vacation months when I took to the trains. Now, every month is a vacation month, and given the state of affairs of our railways, the safer option is air travel, so the romance of train journey had also departed from my life.

Nowadays in Pakistan, in the rail journey, the hours and the days have no relevance. You might plan to reach the destination on Sunday, but the journey could easily stretch to eventual arrival on subsequent Tuesday. This is because it is not in your control and not in the control of clueless railways ministry. A day's journey could, if you are lucky, take only three days. Air-conditioned class tickets don't even provide a fan for comfort, what to talk of AC.

MOIST-EYED

Bookstalls still can be found at most train stations, but timetables are non-existent. They have gone the way of the telephone directory. It is no longer possible to tick off train stations in train timetables or look up numbers in a phone directory.

I was sitting in the Kaifi train and nostalgia had gripped me. Back into the present, here I was on an Indian train, at the Aligarh station. The station of the city, where my father had departed the world, leaving us to say goodbye to Aligarh and clock the journey sans him to our ancestral home in Ghazipur.

I was thinking of the journey my mother would have had to endure and her thoughts as she would have looked out of the train window when leaving behind her deceased husband for safekeeping in the Aligarh Muslim University graveyard and going back to Ghazipur. Surely, she would have been thinking how she would continue the lonely journey ahead with five young kids. Regardless of whether the train moved or not, the matrimonial journey had come to a screeching halt for my mother. Just getting to the destination was no cure for loneliness; that was to be her fate for the rest of her life.

I can't even begin to fathom the pain my mother would have been going through on that journey, battling unimaginable grief and uncertainty. In decades to come, I became witness to her decades of loneliness. I was part of it. It was all etched in my memory, and I could feel the depths of it. I was no longer a two-year-old or a two-feet-tall girl. I could stand on my own. I was privy to her thoughts and griefs. I kept all of that aside and ran to catch my train as I switched back to today.

In my stay of three days at Aligarh. I had tried to cover as much ground as humanly possible. I even stood on the entrance of the house that was built on our very own piece of land. The house named Mishkawa was built on a plot of land that we had owned, but the name plate outside today identified it as the property of someone else. I had stood in front of that house and had cried. If my father had lived to build a house on this plot, I wonder which room would have been mine. Letting my imagination run wild, I was searching for an elusive room that my father never got a chance to build on a plot of land that he rightly owned but never got a chance to lay a claim or a brick on. The built house that stood there now was quite barren and effused a feeling of dread. I was least bothered to care how the building was from inside. When you take land that does not belong to you, then the edifice on it is never welcoming. I did not let my tears drop on that piece of land and dried them in my dupatta. I did not want even my tears on the land, which had been nabbed by ungrateful relatives—long deceased but never forgotten as usurpers.

While I had been aware of this place and its history, I was not obviously aware of its location. Thanks to Hamida Apa and Saeed Bhai, I was able to see this place. They

MOIST-EYED

were my true relatives who were near and dear to me. They were privy to our trials and tribulations and aware of what my tears meant. Holding my hand, Hamida Apa had taken me to another house called Taleem Manzil, a reference to which was also in my father's poetry. I was thus able to see the house where my father had organised an event in honour of my eldest brother when he was eight years old. That date had been 12 October 1936, and none of us other siblings had been born by then. On that day, my father had said:

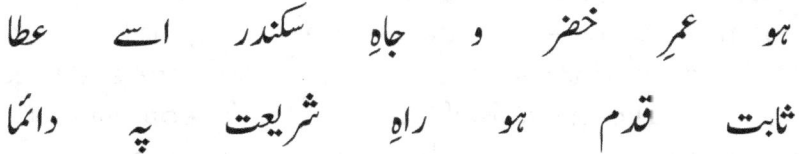

May you have the lifespan of Khizar and the glory of Alexander;
May you remain steadfast on the path of Shariat for eternity.

My eldest brother, Hasan Akhtar, lived a very active and fruitful life until his last breath to the age of 85 years. As the saying goes, he found the life of Sikandar and remained steadfast. He was an accomplished individual who found solace in religion. I had lost him just five months ago. Otherwise, once back in Karachi, I would have dashed to his house and recounted my journey and would have especially mentioned that I had been to the place where our father prayed for him and had him blessed for life.

My tears flowed freely, and I let them run their course. What was the point of restraining them? Tissue papers are useful for tears, not for an avalanche of tears. I left the tears to their own.

I had also visited 2 Marris Road in Aligarh. This was where my father had breathed his last. Commercial development had changed the entire landscape. Gone were the jamun and mango trees and the vines and creepers. Where was the courtyard in which food was cooked, not in pots but in cauldrons—given the number of daily visitors? I am told once my doll had fallen on a log of fire here, and I had cried a lot. I don't know if I had cried on the day when my father lay on the bed at this address, shrouded in white, and when he was lifted and taken to his final resting place.

The train whistled and pulled out of the Aligarh platform.

Aligarh was slipping away from me, again.

I heard similar noises and voices on Indian trains stations to the ones I hear on Pakistani rail stations. People looked the same. Same likes and dislikes. Similar dressing and relatable style of animated talking. Ghalib is Ghalib for all. Iqbal's Tarana is equally acceptable to both nations. Only on land, a line was carved out. Sometimes, this line becomes the dividing line of hate, and other times, it becomes an inviable fence or boundary separating us.

MOIST-EYED

Miles to go before I sleep.

During this late-night journey, I still wanted to catch a glimpse of every train station, but the AC compartment had dual layer of windows, and frost blurred the outside vision.

The legal documentation provided by my cousin sister Bilquis, and her personally accompanying me everywhere, along with her son Azam, had thankfully made the journey bearable and fruitful.

Previously, I had only seen her once when she had visited Pakistan a long time back. She had given an undertaking to the Indian Government for my good conduct during my trip and stay in India.

If crying was a crime, she would have certainly been arrested and jailed as my guarantor, given my poor conduct of shedding tears at every step. If crying was banned, I would never have been able to make this journey. My tears were my treasures that had not been confiscated at any point, and I unashamedly declared them at every stop.

My cousin had rightly suggested that we make use of the night-time to sleep, because there was nothing to see on this train journey, and we would only get to Azamgarh in the morning. However, I'm averse to spending rail trips sleeping. Atlas and geography books point to the mountains, rivers, islands and cities as destination markers, but they do not show the buzz at train stations or the greenery around them, the feeble mud huts on the side of the train tracks, the swathes of farmland and crops swaying in the wind, the grazing animals, the kids racing the trains along the tracks. They can only be seen and enjoyed on a train journey. Thanks to the rail journey, I was getting close by the minute to the city where I was born, Ghazipur—but before that, there was a stopover in Azamgarh.

Azamgarh was my cousin sister's home. She taught at a local school and had taken a leave of absence to come to Delhi to accompany me on this pilgrimage of mine. How could I not be indebted to her? Blood relations trump everything else, even if there is a gap of a few decades between them. After twelve hours' night-time journey and some four to six hours of daytime journey, we eventually got to Azamgarh. Like all other train stations, this was just the same, and I did not necessarily have any direct emotional attachment. But I knew that I would surely have relatives. However, nothing was more important and dearer to me than my cousin sister's house. Azamgarh also has Shibli College and Darul Musannefin Shibli Academy and boasts of many other historical, literary and educational credits.

In Azamgarh, I was suddenly reminded of one person.

Although he taught me for only a few months at the Urdu department at Karachi University; I had found Prof Anjum Azmi to be one of the best professors I ever had the chance to learn from. In later years, we got together often, and he used to visit our home as well. He was an

MOIST-EYED

Alig and also a student of Prof Rasheed Ahmed Siddiqui as well. I was terribly reminded of him when I got to Azamgarh and made a silent prayer for his soul.

My two days' stay here was a display of extraordinary recipe of hospitality. Azam and his wife Shagufta took exceptional care of me. My cousin sister Bilquis would leave me with them as she went back to schoo during the day. Those were crucial days for her, as she was retiring from government post, and her presence was necessary at work to finalise the paperwork. I was surprised that she still had managed to take leave in her last week and had spent that time with me, because per government rules, vacations were not allowed in those last few days. Yet, she had somehow managed that just for me I was truly indebted and always will be.

6

The elaborate imagery I had constructed over the past six decades now lay shattered. At that moment, an unknown sharp object seemed to pierce my heart. It wasn't just my flooded eyes; my entire body was crying out loud, shedding not white transparent tears but red, like blood. It seemed as though I had bled my heart out.

Chapter 6

My Birthplace — Hasan Manzil, Ghazipur

The second most significant destination on my journey was Ghazipur, a city with a history spanning at least 700 years. Its settlement narrative closely mirrors that of the Sindh province. The climatic allure attracted people from distant places, leading to the establishment of educational institutions that played a pivotal role in shaping its rich history. Ghazipur's reputation as one of the most beautiful cities in India was enhanced by the cultivation of roses. Throughout its history, the city hosted eminent rulers, and it served as the birthplace or adopted home for numerous poets and literary giants.

Notably, Ghazipur gained historical prominence as the site of the Third Battle of Buxar. Charles Cornwallis, the former Governor General and Commander-in-Chief of the British Empire in India, who also faced off against the freedom fighter Tipu Sultan, found his final resting place in Ghazipur. Renowned warriors and rulers, including Ashoka, Humayun, Babar, Sher Shah Suri, Gautam Budh, Saleem Shah, Akbar, and Ali Quli Khan, have left their mark on this fertile land. Ghazipur's significance even earned it a mention in the Persian *Ain-e-Akbari*.

The literary and historical significance of Ghazipur experienced a remarkable expansion when Sir Syed Ahmed Khan was transferred from Moradabad to Ghazipur on 3 May 1862. Initially arriving as a sub-judge, he laid the foundation of the Victoria School. On 9 January 1863, along the banks of the Ganga River in Lal Kothi Muhalla Sialpur, the first Scientific Society of India was established, laying the groundwork for the future Aligarh Muslim University.

During his tenure in Ghazipur, Sir Syed Ahmed Khan penned *Tabyin-ul-Kalaam*, a work that aimed to highlight the parallels between Islam and Christianity. Additionally, he compiled *Tarikh-i-Firoz Shahi* and *Tuzk-e-Jahangiri* in Ghazipur. Notably, he undertook the translation of his grandfather's Persian book *Fawaid AlAfkar Fi Alamal AlFarja* into Urdu and had it published in Ghazipur.

A noteworthy event during Sir Syed's time in Ghazipur was the wedding of his son, for which Maulana Farooq Chriakoti composed a khutba. What makes this particularly significant is that the khutba was written without a single word featuring a dot.

Subsequently, the Sir Syed Ahmed Memorial Fund Committee, led by Nawab Mohsin ul Mulk, also made its way to Ghazipur. The pivotal meeting took place in

MOIST-EYED

Samad Manzil. Molvi Abdul Samad, my great-grandfather and the brother of the accomplished Urdu and Persian poet Hafiz Qadri Muhammad Ali, played a significant role in this context. Sir Syed Ahmed Khan corresponded extensively with Molvi Abdul Samad, with more than two dozen letters addressed to Samad Manzil in Ghazipur. Unfortunately, the fate of these letters after the partition of the Subcontinent remains unknown, marking yet another loss attributed to that period.

Molvi Abdul Samad also contributed to the literary landscape by publishing the **Aina Tehzeeb** magazine, a precursor to Urdu journalism, holding substantial historical significance. In Ghazipur, the conducive environment fostered the flourishing of education and literary pursuits, attracting a plethora of poets, educationists, literary giants and scholars.

Ghazipur was further honoured by the presence of Rabindranath Tagore, the first Indian Nobel Prize-winning poet, whose influence has solidified the city's reputation for years to come. Tagore resided in Ghazipur until 1888, drawn to the city by its renowned roses. Even in those times, Ghazipur was acknowledged as the City of Roses, and Tagore was aware of the exportation of these roses to Asia and Europe. Seeking solace in this serene, delightful, and fragrant city, Tagore composed some of his early works.

It was amidst the open air and tranquil surroundings of Ghazipur that he penned the song **Darwish Ka Piyasa** and twenty-eight other notable poems. His poetry collection *Manasi* was compiled here, and the ambience of Ghazipur is credited for inspiring his first mature work. However, it was his collection *Gitanjali* that catapulted him to global fame.

In addition to Tagore, the Sufi poet Malik Muhammad Jayasi also graced Ghazipur. Jayasi is renowned for composing the epic poem *Padmawat*.

Imprisoned until 1920 in Malta, Sheikh-ul-Hind Maulana Mehmood ul Hasan, chose Ghazipur as his home upon his return. Subsequently, Maulana Hussain Ahmed Madni also graced the city with his presence and made it his abode. At its zenith, the city boasted twenty-two educational institutions, fifty-three madrassas and over two hundred mosques. The rich educational and cultural tapestry of Ghazipur attracted people from far and wide, turning it into a centre of learning and creativity. Notably, it is home to two world-class and globally renowned madrasas: Chashm-e-Rahmat and Madrasa Dinia.

Although Fort William College was established in Calcutta, its founder, the renowned linguist John Gilchrist, resided in Ghazipur before that. It was in Ghazipur that he compiled and authored the English-Hindustani dictionary.

Ghazipur has been a cradle of talent, nurturing the educational journeys of writers such as Syed Sajjad Haider Yaldram and Al-e-Ahmed Saroor. Satirical poet Akhbar Allahabadi and essayist-biographer Kazi Abdul Wadud also

MOIST-EYED

produced landmark works during their time in Ghazipur. Dr Abdul Aleem, hailing from Ghazipur, went on to become the chancellor of Aligarh Muslim University, with the city contributing five vice-chancellors to the institution.

The city has also given birth to notable figures like Mumtaz Hussain, Rahi Masoom Raza and Ali Abbas Husseini. Muhammad Ali Jouhar, the famous son of Bi Amma, was brought up here. Ghazipur was witness to Begum Attiya Faizi's campaign against purdah, with my grandmother reciting a poem in opposition during her jalsa. Unfortunately, the survival of that nazm was another casualty of the partition.

Adding to the city's significance, Syed Ahmed Shaheed Barelvi illuminated Ghazipur with his arrival. Seven Shuhada of Balakot hailed from this city, and their names are etched on the tomb of Syed Ahmed Shaheed.

In my mind, the history of Ghazipur unfolded like scenes from a documentary film. For decades, I had heard tales of this city, and now, finally, I found myself blessed with the opportunity to revisit my birthplace. The journey from Azamgarh to Ghazipur took nearly two hours, and with every passing moment, my anticipation grew. As we approached Ghazipur, my heartbeat quickened in tandem with the realisation that awaited me.

Upon my arrival in Ghazipur, the harsh reality struck me hard. Despite having owned significant portions of land here just a generation ago, I, as an empty-handed visitor, had no legal claim to any piece of it. The weight of this truth brought tears, left my body limp and caused my lips to tremble. I questioned whether I could muster the strength to continue.

Lost in contemplation, the car came to a stop and parked. Before me stood Hasan Manzil and Samad Manzil.

A mere few steps separated me from the entrance to Hasan Manzil, whose last undisputed legal owners were my parents. The fate of the property at the time of partition—who seized it, and who occupied it—remained unknown. The details of the transaction—who sold it on our behalf and to whom—were shrouded in mystery. The sole victim of this opaque transaction was the rightful legal owner, my widowed mother. Until her last breath, she harboured deep sentiments for this place. It was the house where she entered as a bride, where she gave birth to seven children, mourned the loss of two and departed abruptly as a widow with five young children in tow. Although she was the undisputed legal heir to the property, the absence of my father left no avenue to assert our claim. Our house, our money, our inheritance—we never had the chance to possess or appreciate any of it.

Guided gently towards the entrance, I took my first step inside, and a peculiar electric charge seemed to course through my body—painful yet rejuvenating. A sudden shriek escaped me, likely drawing the attention of those few who were nearby. Silently, I cried out, "Hasan Manzil is mine, and I stand here as its rightful owner."

MOIST-EYED

Perhaps I lacked a legal land title to present in a human court of law, but that did not alter the fundamental truth.

In that moment, I felt incredibly feeble.

Before me stood a frail woman within the entrance of the dilapidated house. Perhaps she sensed the return of the original owner to reclaim her property, or perhaps not. Regardless, her demeanour held no animosity only a genuine smile as she warmly welcomed me inside. She took my arm and hurriedly ushered me into a small, broken room.

However, this couldn't be THE room. THE room, where I was born, was described as vast and expansive, boasting a total of six doors. I had come into this world in a corner master bed within that mansion-sized room. Eager to locate it, I wanted to run around swiftly. I envisioned finding a steel suitcase perched on the wall, where my doll, colouring book and pencil with a rubber top awaited me. Perhaps the doll had cried itself to sleep in my absence, but I hoped my pencil and colouring book would still be there to offer companionship. The urgency to retrieve my cherished belongings overwhelmed me, yet it seemed that I couldn't move, let alone run. My legs gave way, and I felt paralyzed. I tried to use my eyes to scan and capture my surroundings, but tears blurred my vision. Even as I struggled to reach for my dupatta to wipe away my tears, it appeared to have lost its absorbent quality.

A few children had materialised seemingly out of nowhere, standing around me, while some elders observed from a distance. In that moment, I preferred to imagine that I was surrounded by my siblings and parents, transported back to happier times. Did I see my mom, beaming with joy and excitement in a way I had never seen before? The illusion, however, dissipated almost as quickly as it had appeared. Once again, I found myself alone.

Sensing the possibility of my stumbling during this emotional rollercoaster, the frail woman offered me strength, holding onto me as she extended an invitation to explore the place. However, in its current state of disrepair, there was hardly anything noteworthy to see. The Hasan Manzil I had grown up hearing and imagining was now reduced to ruins, dilapidated to the nth degree. Not a single room was complete or habitable. In the open lounge, an open sewer flowed across the mud ground—a stark contrast to the necessity it once served in bygone Indian houses. Witnessing this in the present day, with pungent water flowing, was deeply disconcerting.

Amidst this experience, I was reminded of Lord Tennyson's poem, **The Brook**, a piece we had studied in school that remains etched in my mind. It encapsulates the bittersweet blend of the fleeting nature of human life and the enduring resilience of nature.

'For men may come and men may go,

But I go on forever.'

I carefully hopped over the open sewer, encountering a broken-down remnant of a wall in front of it. The rooms inside appeared to have been pulled down, a stark departure from the imagery I had envisioned in my mind.

A wave of genuine guilt washed over me for my inadequacy and the inability to reverse time and restore the mansion to its former glory.

There is a saying that it's not just humans who love their homes, but houses also warm up to their inhabitants when treated well. If I were to undertake the task of rebuilding this place, I had heard enough stories to be able to recreate the floor plan in my mind.

I mentioned to those around me that there used to be a barcha. They assured me it was still there, and I was led to that part of the house. However, once again, I faced disappointment as it bore no resemblance to how I had been told or I had imagined. Despite this, I recognised the road just outside.

I was reminded that I used to stand on a stool to watch the Muharram processions passing by that road. During the ten days of Muharram, we would receive stringed cloth purses filled with dry fruits, a treat we enjoyed sharing with friends. Hasan Manzil, our home, was elevated, allowing us to peek down at the passing processions. My grandmother, recognising the universal significance of Imam Hussain and Muharram, used to financially contribute to these processions. Although I did not participate in the matam, I felt a profound sadness.

I doubted whether the processions, once funded with my grandmother's finances, still passed by the house. I wished to meet the organisers, eager to contribute on behalf of my late grandmother and revive that tradition.

The lower portion of the house was desolate and bare. There were no rooms, no hallways, no kitchen, and no brass pitchers, silver cups and flowered pots. The room of my birth was nowhere to be found, and with it vanished the steel suitcase perched by the wall, where my doll, colouring book and pencil with a rubber top should have been.

I encountered the staircase that used to lead us to the top floor, guarded by a door that had clearly seen better days. I was informed that once, I had my finger stuck in the bolt of that door. I had cried for an extended period, prompting all the servants and maids to rush to my aid. Despite their efforts, my finger had become horribly stuck, and it was only my mom who managed to use oil to extricate it from the bolt. As I placed my hand on that very bolt, I found solace in this small remnant from days gone by. It was an innocent attempt on my part to bridge the gap between two eras by touching that bolt.

Yet, time, like the two sides of a river, often remains unbridged. Have those sides ever truly met? While I was careful not to fear getting my finger stuck again, my caution was different. I realised that if it did get stuck and I cried, there was no longer a mother who could come

MOIST-EYED

running to my rescue. Nor were my two faithful private helpers, Hanif and Rafee, who were once assigned to me, around anymore. I recalled them both—not their faces, but certainly their names. While their children might still be in the city, the task of finding them seemed insurmountable.

The upper portion of the house was reserved for my grandfather. He spent his days studying and writing there, but my faint recollections bring back evenings when he sat serenely in his distinctive armchair, dressed in white. From a distance, he looked like an angel from a faraway land, and to me, there was no one more beautiful.

This man held prominent positions in the Indian Educational Service, serving on all major educational posts. In the garden cultivated by Sir Syed Ahmed Khan, he was friends with the glittering flowers and jewels of individuals like Nawab Muzzamilullah Khan, Nawab Ismail Khan, Nawab Mohsin ul Mulk, Waqar ul Mulk, Sir Suleman Ashraf, Sir Dr Ziauddin and Nawab Habib Ur Rehman Sherwani. He was a patron of numerous religious and educational institutions.

This was my grandfather's house and my father's house. While my father brought intellectual brilliance and honesty, he forgot to bring a long life with him.

As his daughter, I pondered why I had come to see his house after six decades. I lacked a concise or straightforward answer for that.

As I ascended the stairs, the pristine and gentle image of my grandfather's space became vivid in my memory. However, what awaited me upstairs was nothing like I had imagined. There was nothing remotely resembling my recollections; instead, it was a scene of sheer dilapidation and desolate misery. Time and neglect had taken their toll, erasing everything. Where were the once neatly arranged books and papers? The daily cleaned courtyard was nowhere to be found, and the elite of Ghazipur who used to frequent the place were absent. Yet, these details persisted in my memory, and I was determined to hold onto them.

On the walls, stone ledges indicated the spots where cupboards used to be. No doors remained, and the wooden ledges had turned black. There used to be a wooden takht with white side pillows where my grandfather would sit with their support. As I paced around, I wondered if it used to be here. I stood still, reminiscing about the evening he gave me a *Khilona* magazine. Although I couldn't read, he had it subscribed in my name. All I recalled was the picture of the Iron Man, which I eagerly searched for in every magazine. Clad in a chequered shirt, he appeared robust, possessing the strength to endure the toughest challenges without a scratch, while the other things around him would crumple. My grandfather used to narrate this story and concluded by advising me to start reading myself. I only had the chance to glimpse a few magazines before partition deprived me of this too.

I remembered Iron Man, but there was no one around to complete the rest of the story. *Khilona* magazine did eventually make its way to Pakistan, but sadly, it was without the presence of the Iron Man. Somewhere in the chaos of partition, even Iron Man slipped through the cracks. When I began writing, I turned to crafting short stories. How I wished I could recite them to my grandfather. Surely, he would have been immensely proud and happy for me, right?

To that question, I had no answer. There was no wooden takht, no grandfather and no *Khilona*. It was at this point that I experienced such a sudden bout of dizziness. If there hadn't been people around to support me, I could have become the first casualty from the roof of Hasan Manzil.

After a few hours of reflection, I bid farewell to Hasan Manzil, and the following Urdu couplet by Faiz Ahmed Faiz came to mind.

دونوں جہاں تیری محبت میں ہار کی
وہ جا رہا ہے کوئی شب غم گزار کے

Lost both the worlds in the quest for your love;
There he goes, leaving a night of grief in his wake.

This evening, filled with a blend of sadness and pain, took an even more poignant turn. The elaborate imagery I had constructed over the past six decades now lay shattered. At that moment, an unknown sharp object seemed to pierce my heart. It wasn't just my flooded eyes; my entire body was crying out loud, shedding not white transparent tears but red, like blood. It seemed as though I had bled my heart out. Today, I was surrendering Hasan Manzil.

I don't know how I managed to step down and out of the house. My eyes were clouded with tears, and I couldn't see properly. Under my breath, I uttered, "Hasan Manzil, today I surrender and give up my claim over you."

Outside, Samad Manzil stood tall.

This property, too, had belonged to my grandfather. Between 1862 and 1864, Sir Syed Ahmed Khan used to reside here. My grandfather Molvi Abdul Samad and Hafiz Qari Muhammad Ali were poets who wrote in both Urdu and Persian, representing the nobility of Ghazipur. My grandfather also had an acquaintance with Mirza Ghalib and had the honour of sharing his poetry with him.

Upon entering Samad Manzil, a sudden rush of pride enveloped me. When ancestors leave a positive legacy, it can provide future generations with comfort, inspiration and pride, as I felt today. In this house, my relative Akhtar Bhai's son Ubaidur Rehman Siddiqui resides. He authored the *History of Ghazipur* and the *Tazkara Mashaik of Ghazipur*, gaining international fame. He also

MOIST-EYED

wrote *Ghazipur Literary Pasmanzar* and serves as a professor of English at a local college, prolifically writing in Urdu as well. Although younger than me, he has garnered numerous accolades and accomplishments. During my visit to Ghazipur, he graciously hosted me.

As a writer accustomed to wielding the pen, Ubaid was adept at reading the writings of the heart. He showed me incredible respect in his house and gave me a tour. While the tides of time had taken their toll on Samad Manzil, having my relatives living there ensured that some rooms and relics from the past had survived. When your own people inhabit a house, it thrives. Hasan Manzil and Samad Manzil stood in stark contrast to each other, despite sharing a common history.

The next day, Ubaid had arranged a gathering of the literary heavyweights of the city. He went the extra mile, printing a banner in my honour, appointing me as the chief guest and orchestrating a Mushaira. This evening of 28 May turned out to be truly memorable, and I remain grateful to Ubaid for making it special. Following that, I had just one more evening left in this city.

The subsequent evening became unforgettable due to the presence of some very special people.

Ubaid had extended invitations to well-known and talented poets. Aziz Ghazipuri, a larger-than-life personality adorned in a crisp white kurta, presided over the Mushaira. Other notable poets included the esteemed

Badshah sahab, Nazar Ghazipuri, Nafees Alam and Rais Shahidi, with Saif ur Rehman sahab conducting the proceedings.

During my forty-year tenure at Allama Iqbal Girls Degree College Karachi, where I served both as a professor and later as the principal, I had the privilege of hosting more than forty mushairas. Over the years, the popularity of these events in Karachi soared, garnering exceptional coverage in the local press. Newspaper columns were dedicated to them, and they became a topic of discussion in private literary circles. The calibre of poets and their poetry, the meticulous organisation, the discipline of the students and their refined appreciation of the poets, which I coached them on, became talk of the town.

Renowned author and poet Shabnam Romani was a regular attendee at these Mushaira gatherings. In one of his columns for the Urdu daily **Mashriq**, he wrote, "If you want to experience or present poetry in a peaceful, disciplined, and enthusiastic environment, if you desire due praise, an exceptional welcome and respect for yourself, then participate in the mushairas at Allama Iqbal Girls Degree College." This comment was heartening for both me and my students.

Throughout the year, discussions about the Mushaira lingered, and poets eagerly awaited the next year's event. If a particular poet was not invited one year, complaints would persist, and I had to manage the fallout.

MOIST-EYED

As I sat in this intimate and exclusive Mushaira gathering, I was reminded of my college Mushairas, where poets numbered around twenty to twenty-five with over thousand attendees.

The stage was adorned with such elegance that it rivalled a bride's wedding stage. However, this small yet distinguished gathering of poets in my honour, orchestrated by Akhtar Bhai's genuineness, Ubaid's affection and the kindness of accomplished poets who attended on short notice, left an indelible mark on my memory in a very pleasant manner. Though I was originally from this city, but was my past. My present status was that of a tourist. To still be celebrated here, in this way was truly exhilarating.

In the audience, among others, was my dear cousin Bilquis. However, there was another fascinating individual present; Mr Ram G Kesri, a perfume expert. Like myself, Ram G Kesri was not a poet, but he relished being associated with mushairas. As we neared the end of the gathering, he was given an opportunity to address us. He said that he wasn't a poet but rather a trader of fragrances; capturing everyone's attention with this statement. The line itself seemed worthy of a poem. While elaborating on the significance of Ghazipur and roses, he generously gifted each of us a small vial of rose scent that he had crafted with his own hands.

According to him, it takes 1 mann (almost 40 kg) of rose petals to fill a mere 2-inch bottle with 100% pure extract, costing around INR 20,000. He dismissed the market-sold versions as adulterated, acknowledging that not many can afford pure rose extract. However, he conceded that the adulterated version is potent enough for the fragrance to linger even after a few washes of clothes. Considering this, the potency of the pure version is beyond imagination.

I had the chance to lace a few drops on my sleeves. The fragrance instantly filled the room, competing with the lingering scent of the poets and their poetry. Overwhelmed, I said to Mr Ram G Kesri, "Who would be irresponsible enough to ever wash this cloth again?"

He thoroughly enjoyed this comment. Later on, he demonstrated the application of khewra in a manner akin to a magician's sleight of hands and wizardry. Mr Kesri called for a transparent glass filled with water. Taking out a needle from a small bottle of khewra, he dipped it in the water and claimed that the entire water content was now khewra. We smelled the water and agreed that it indeed smelled of khewra.

His demonstrations added a rich colour to the gathering. I didn't want the session to end; after all, it was my first interaction here with its inhabitants in such a long time.

Even though they had heard stories over the decades and had anecdotes to share about Hasan Manzil, none had any mention of my family, as we had been displaced

MOIST-EYED

from here very early on. I made an effort to capture each and every member in the gathering in the memory of my eyes. I believe I succeeded, because even today, when I close my eyes, I can see them. The quality of poetry that night was sublime. It felt gratifying to know that somehow, somewhere, the atmosphere of this city still preserves its historical roots of literature and poetry.

In the end, as per tradition, the nazim asked me to recite some poetry. What could I say? I told them that my kalaam had been stolen. They all expressed concern for my loss. I quipped that Allama Iqbal had stolen my kalaam and made it his own. They all laughed. One poet said, "Well, you must remember the kalaam, so do say something from it."

I read this couplet:

اپنے من میں ڈوب کر پا جا سراغِ زندگی
تُو اگر میرا نہیں بنتا نہ بن اپنا تو بن

Delve into your soul to seek the clues for the purpose of life;
If you cannot find me, at least discover yourself.

I doubt if even Allama Iqbal would have received as much praise for it as I did.

Thereafter I spoke about a lot of other things about Pakistan—literary events, poets from there, my favourite people, the style of living, style of speaking, education and learning, my college—and they all listened with rapt attention. Then, they surprised me with their kindness as, one after another, a person would get up and put Marigold flower necklaces around my neck. Akhtar bhai and Ubaid wanted me to wear many of these flower necklaces. I wondered about the merit of my importance that equated to such an awesome reception.

Many people we meet for the first time, without any prior relationship, remain an indelible part of our memory forever. They cannot be forgotten. These people were the same. They were people of my city. I was meeting them for the first time and probably for the last time.

Unfortunately, the evening had to come to an end. I gave them some of my books, and Ubaid gave me his book. These book gifts are priceless. We pass away, but these books remain on the shelf, in our collection. The author and the readers die, but the book survives. It is true that what is written survives.

Looking over from Samad Manzil to see Hasan Manzil shrouded in darkness, I wished I could have grown up in that house, with all its glory intact. I wished I could have stayed in Ghazipur forever, with my family by my side. I would have devoured all the books in the library of Hasan Manzil. I have always wondered what happened to all those books. Those were invaluable, priceless collections, but I don't know who the authors were, who ended up securing them and where they would be today. Where did it all go? Or did they get destroyed in some rains or floods? Oh! Why did I not come to save them sooner? The shrieks of the abandoned books were unbearable for me. I clasped my hands on my ears and turned away from Hasan Manzil, surrendering yet once again to the misfortunes.

That night was indeed a typical Ghazipur night. There was no electricity, and the weather and even the water were quite hot. However, I was oblivious to such inconveniences. Later that night, I relived the Mushaira again in my mind. I was never going to be able to scratch this from my memory until my last breath; not that many decades are left to go, anyway. I am simply aiming to transcribe this memory into writing for my coming generations. I am hopeful—and also not too hopeful—that it will last forever. My kids have migrated. The past is being forgotten.

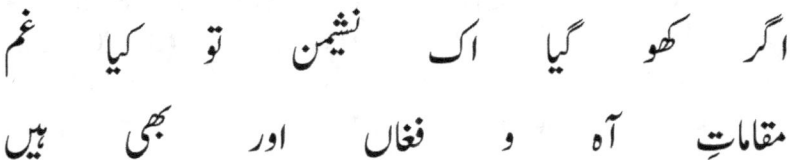

What is there to grieve if residence is lost;
There are more occasions to cry and sigh for.

The new generation has a different approach to remembering or forgetting. While my books rest on a shelf in our home, my kids are building their lives in distant foreign lands. I am hopeful that one day, they will return to their roots, having conquered the world. They might discover my books, possibly gathering dust, and by fate or fortune, may decide their fate. Perhaps the furniture will also be discarded, and who knows, even our home, Noor Ghar, might be put up for sale. The fate of our home might follow the path of Hasan Manzil. Nothing in life is eternal, and this process of fading away is a sobering reality.

In Ghazipur, there were many places to explore, but time was not on my side. The scorching heat and relentless power outages didn't make things any easier. However, the storm in my heart and mind kept urging me to visit and see as much as I could.

One such place was Madrasa Dinia, and another was Madrasa Chashm-e-Rahmat.

Both these educational institutions were established and financially supported by my elders. Madrasa Dinia came into existence in the third decade of the 20th century, and its inaugural event took place on 15 February 1936. At that time, my father was a young man of thirty-one. While there were renowned intellectuals and religious scholars in Ghazipur, my father, as the president of the reception committee, shouldered the responsibility of delivering the presidential address.

MOIST-EYED

This speech was printed and circulated, and by chance, I have been incredibly fortunate to possess a copy of that publication.

I could not have even dreamed that one day I would step into Madrasa Dinia and, if I did, be remembered as the daughter of the young man who delivered the first presidential address at this esteemed institution. However, fate works in mysterious ways and led me there.

By the grace of Allah, not only does Madrasa Dinia still exist, but it also continues to work tirelessly in furthering religious education.

In every suburb or village, big or small, there are more than half a dozen madrasas established, and the current administrator is Azizul Hasan Siddiqui sahab. He is not only a religious scholar but also the author of many books. I had already read one of his books, **Mashaheer-e-Ghazipur**.

Now that I was in the same city, meeting him was a must. I had gone to Madrasa Dinia to search for my father and grandfather's footprints, and as luck would have it, I met Aziz ul Hasan Siddiqui sahab. Until then, I was not aware that he was the administrator of Madrasa Dinia as well.

When I saw him for the first time, his radiant personality and charisma made me feel like lowering my head in reverence to him. Clad in crisp, clean white clothes, with a flowing white beard and a white cap, Aziz sahab was truly living up to his name, which meant, dear. I was introduced by Ubaid, but soon, Aziz sahab started asking me direct questions and took over the introduction, as he knew each and every member of my paternal side, be it my father or grandfather. He was fully aware of their achievements and knew more about their involvement here than I did. In his eyes, I could see the silhouettes of my father and grandfather. He informed me of the invaluable financial and non-financial support that they had provided in getting Madrasa Dinia started. Later, he took me to the Abul Hasan Library, named after his father. I told him that I might consider it as my grandfather's library, since he too had the same name. He smiled with pleasure.

In the library, he asked me to look closely in a showcase, and I was pleasantly surprised to see a presidential address document. "This is my father's! Saved here?" I was both astonished and pleased. My coming here was nothing less than a miracle. Fate was bringing me closer to my own people. Thanking the Almighty for the blessings is already due upon us, but in those moments while standing, I had already fallen in prostration. My father's handwritten documents were saved here. Man is impermanent, but things endure. Reputation and achievements survive. The tears that welled up were of happiness, and I dedicated them to my father.

"Azizul Hasan sahab, what have you shown me! Incredibly grateful that you have preserved this."

There was apparently more to astonish me with. I was handed over a visitor register in which there were comments from very reputable, larger-than-life personalities. I started reading those, but Azizul Hasan sahab said it is not merely for reading; he wanted me to ink my own comments in it as well.

In the unbearable heat, my body literally froze. The quick scan of the names of those who had penned their thoughts; I just couldn't bring myself to be in that league.

On Azizul Hasan sahab's insistence or desire, or maybe just to ease my heart, he chose to bestow that honour. It was not just with a pen but with my emotions and tears I scribbled a few lines, which now completely escape my memory.

Life at times throws up such unrivalled moments, without asking. I savoured, relished and stored them in my heart, my eyes and my thoughts. Given how stretched I was for time, it was nonetheless a very rewarding experience and meeting. I received another copy of the book **Mashaheer-e-Ghazipur** and some magazines focusing on the efforts and achievements of Madrasa Dinia. The meeting left me yearning for more time at the Madrasa. Who knows if our time is up soon afterwards

After my return to Karachi, his memory lingers vividly. The aura of his personality continues to surprise me. There is a quarterly monthly magazine published in Lucknow. He had given me the Oct–Dec 2013 and Jan–June 2014 issues, which I brought along without having a chance to read. When I finally got around to opening and reading them, I found articles published on my grandfather Molvi Abdul Samad and Hafiz Qari Muhammad Ali in both. The article on Qari Muhammad Ali is by Maulana Saud Al Hasan, the son of Maulana Azizul Hasan sahab, bearing a striking resemblance to his illustrious father. The article on Molvi Abdul Samad is by Maulana Shakoor Alam, whom I missed out on meeting at the Madrasa. What a lovely coincidence that in the very month I reached Ghazipur, there is an article about my own ancestors in that quarter's publication. This cannot be mere coincidence but something more profound—fate at play.

Another incredibly amazing thing was another write-up sent my way after my return to Karachi. It was a write-up about the 5th annual function of Madrasa Dinia, held on 26–28 April 1952. The presidential address had been delivered by Anwar Ul Hasan sahab, Municipal Commissioner at that time. This was the fifth address since my father's inaugural one. The shocking piece in the write-up was my grandfather's apparent speech at the event, and his comments were recorded therein and remain preserved to this day. I am reproducing them so that the preservation may continue via my travelogue as well. With the write-up is the thanks of the organisers as well, which goes as follows: "We are especially grateful to Molvi Haji Abul Hasan sahab, IES Retired, who not only attended each and every session from start to finish but also wrote his opinions for us."

MOIST-EYED

I would have remained unaware of this document if Azizul Hasan sahab had not kindly unearthed it and sent me a photocopy. In moments like these, phrases like thank you seem inadequate to convey the depth of gratitude. When I did call him to express my profound thanks, he shared how people in Ghazipur used to call my father a twin in terms of looks to Maulana Abul Kalaam Azad. They both had the same rosy complexion, sherwani, cap and style of beard. Perhaps the distinguished individuals of that era shared a common appearance.

Azizul Hasan sahab, over the phone, mentioned a gathering at his house when my grandfather was migrating to Pakistan. His father had hosted that gathering for my grandfather, both of whom shared the same name. The insistence was that they should at least share one last meal together. On that occasion, his father had recited a Persian nazm. While the nazm was lost in the sands of time, he remembered one couplet that he recited. Due to too much disturbance on the line and the couplet being in Persian, I could not fully comprehend it.

However, I specifically inquired about the Ghazipur graveyard. I was searching for the graves of my 14-year-old uncle and my 14-year-old deceased sister. I had doubts about whether their graves would still be there. To my surprise, Azizul Hasan sahab informed me that he remembered seeing a grave next to a relative of his, Hakim Waliuddin, on which my grandfather's name was mentioned as the relative of the deceased. Naturally, I insisted that he visit the graveyard and let me know if the graves are still there.

Efforts were made to locate the graves, but land grabbers had obliterated all traces, and houses were constructed in the area. I am certain the grave Azizul Hasan sahab saw belonged to either my uncle or my sister. My grandfather was a father to one and a grandfather to the other, both of whom are buried in Pakistan. My father rests in Aligarh, and the final resting places of my uncle and sister remain unknown. Even after visiting their city, I couldn't stand next to their graves. I express my gratitude to the Aligarh graveyard, which has prevented my father from fading into oblivion, allowing me to stand beside him even after so many decades.

Leaving Madrasa Dinia, where I witnessed firsthand their accomplishments over the decades, I was convinced that this is undoubtedly a place on Earth where those associated with it will collectively journey to Jannah. Their transition from this world will be a direct route to Jannat ul Firdous. I pray that this is indeed the case, and I hope to be among them.

The information about Madrasa Dinia that I gathered on my return trip is as follows: Established in 1350 Hijra by Molana Umer Farooq, the educational institution offers Arabic, Hifz or Tajweed, primary education, junior section, girls' high school, coaching for girls, children's home, and various philanthropic or charitable departments, including dawah and printing, ifta ma_lis shariah Dinia Academy, mobile library, Maulana Abul Hasan Library, computer section, society reformation committee, Wifaq Madrasa Islamia, department for the burial of unclaimed dead bodies, summer Islamic camp, Islamic hostel, department for social welfare, and others. It has ten direct branches with around twenty-eight affiliates or associates. Two publications, *Tazkeer and Religion* and *Deen-o-Dawat* are printed, and an annual publication called *Aghahi* is also published. The institution has approximately forty-eight teaching and publication staff members, five individuals dedicated to dawah, twelve non-teaching staff and thirty-eight affiliated teachers. The student body comprises around 2,300 students, with twenty-five residing in the hostel. Arabic and Quran Hifz are compulsory, and the cost up to class 6 is approximately thirty-nine lakh Indian rupees. The Madrasa is not government-funded and relies on charitable donations from the local community.

The other madrasa was Chashma-e-Rahmat, and I was quite eager to visit it, given the stories I had heard throughout my life. I learned that my eldest brother received his early education there, fortunate to study under Maulana Umer Farooq at this madrasa. Numerous learned scholars contributed to the prestige of this institution since its establishment in 1869 by Maulana Rehmatullah Farangi Mehalli. The present building is a mere echo of its past majesty. Graduates of this seminary made significant contributions that brought pride to Ghazipur, leaving an indelible mark in history. Standing at the front gate, my head held high in pride and my eyes lowered in respect, I reflected on the anecdotes and stories shared by my relatives. It reaffirmed the importance of passing down such stories from parents to children, as the past provides strength to the present and comfort to the future.

Inwardly, I felt a profound sense of contentment. Despite my lack of knowledge and understanding, I couldn't help but express my feelings once again:

Glory be to your forefathers indeed, but what of you?

However, merely reaching this point was an accomplishment in itself. Having lived a full life, at this stage, what more could one expect than the natural wear and tear of limbs?

There have been moments when I contemplated leaving behind all worldly pursuits and dedicating myself to such noble institutions. Azizul Hasan sahab is undeniably paving his way to Jannah through the commendable work he is engaged in. I pray that he includes me in his prayers. Recognising my own weaknesses and worldly attachments, my eyes welled up with tears, but for once, I managed to keep them from spilling over. They say the

MOIST-EYED

most challenging task is to halt the tears or draw back those already flooded into the eyes.

As Mir said:

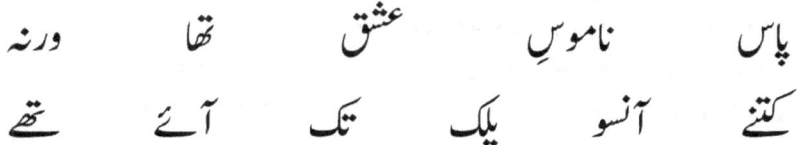

Were it not regard for the dignity of love;
Scores of tears stayed put at the eyelids.

The time designated for my visit to Ghazipur was drawing to a close, and there remained much more that I wished to explore. I had a desire to visit Ameer Masood's grave, a place that I've heard still exists. I wanted to pay my respects to him, acknowledging his efforts in laying the foundation of this city built on the principles of justice. I also had a complaint, feeling that I hadn't received my due share of justice. Nevertheless, I wanted to express gratitude, as it was from the soil of this city that my grandfather and great-grandfather emerged, were nurtured and are still remembered and revered. This city provided them with respect, the pinnacle of glory and an enduring legacy in the annals of history. It is from that generation that we proudly claim our existence, and it is this soil that continues to shelter *Ganjaha-e-Granmaya* for eternity.

With one fateha, I attempted to bless all.

I also had the desire to visit another Mazar known as Zubda Ibada O Arab, and the person resting there was Hafiz Hakeem Habibullah Makki. Originally from Makkah, his ancestor had settled in Ghazipur four hundred years ago. He was renowned for wearing perfumed clothes, swaying in earnest passion and being often immersed in an altered state of trance and consciousness. Known for being a man of his word, executing promises was his trademark quality and well-known virtue. There were tales of him being spotted at two different places simultaneously, and, even more incredulously, there were verified accounts of him being seen at three different places simultaneously. Some people claimed to have seen him praying at the City Mosque of Ghazipur, while others saw him in Mohalla Nooruddin. He passed away on 6 September 1940. I was inspired and curious to visit his Mazar not only because of his remarkable personality but also because the epitaph on his Mazar is Qata Wafat Tarikh, done by my father.

This nazm had seventeen couplets, which are engraved on his Mazar. I wanted to visit, but paucity of time limited my movement.

Another place I could have gone to was Goji Tarka Kanya Patshala, which is where I went to study for a few days as well and is now a girl's college.

MOIST-EYED

Victoria School, founded by Sir Syed Ahmed Khan, still exists, and it is the place where my father first raised the Muslim League flag. While there were numerous other places on my list to visit, one stood out—the residence of a relative by the Ganges River. It was there that I had once purchased mud toys crafted from the Ganges mud. Despite my efforts to find them in Hasan Manzil, just like my parents, grandparents and my first pencil and book; those toys eluded me. Perhaps they would have tried to locate me when I had left abruptly.

And here I am now, back in the city, still searching for them.

7

I hadn't noticed until then, for at that time, I was in a season beyond the four seasons. I do not know how to name that fifth season. Then I realised that it maybe was the season of pain. For my entire body was aching physically and mentally.

Chapter 7

My Ancestral Village — Pehtia

How can I leave out mentioning my ancestral village, Pehtia!

In history books, it's also referred to as Saroli. Back in Pakistan, one of the finest varieties of mangoes is called Saroli. Aromatic and rich in look and taste, perhaps quite like Pehtia of the yore. They say Pehtia used to be a lush green village with an abundance of lakes, farmlands, parks and gardens.

One of the most famous families from here was the family of Sheikh Siddiqui. I am proud to be a descendant of this very family.

Molvi Siddiq had two able sons. One was Hafiz Qari Muhammad Ali. He was well versed in religious and contemporary education and was a well-regarded lawyer all over India. He was also an accomplished poet with Urdu and Persian diwans. While manuscripts of his Urdu poetry did not survive, his Persian poetry fortunately did survive and was published in Aligarh in 1931 under the title *Kulliyat-e-Qari*. The poem that he wrote on Sheikh-ul-Hind Maulana Mahmood-ul-Hasan is legendary.

The other son one was Molvi Abdul Samad. He was a close friend of Sir Syed Ahmed Khan and one of the very first ones to financially contribute towards setting up Aligarh Muslim University. Despite relocating from Ghazipur, Sir Syed continued to correspond with Molvi Abdul Samad and used to stay in Samad Manzil on his visits to the city.

Erudite and a famous jurist, Molvi Abdul Samad was awarded titled of Khan Bahadur by the British Raj, which out of sheer patriotism, he declined to accept. He was also an accomplished poet in both Urdu and Persian, but his manuscripts did not seem to have survived. However, history books do evidence the greatness of his poetry having received praise from Ghalib as well as his close poetic association with Abdul Aleem Aasi Ghazi, about whom Ghalib had remarked, "Praise be to Allah that such poetic geniuses still exist in Hindustan."

Both brothers had constructed houses next to each other in Ghazipur. Hafiz Qari Muhammad Ali also built Haleema Manzil and Muhammad Ali Manzil in Pehtia, which were regarded as architectural masterpieces. I wanted to see whatever remained of both these ancestral homes of mine.

In Pehtia, there lived the well know family of Dr Abdul Aleem Siddiqui, who later on became vice chancellor of Aligarh Muslim University as well. He was our uncle. His house was also in Pehtia, and I wanted to visit it as well.

Fatima Manzil was also something I wanted to pay a visit to, which belonged to my uncle, Junaid Alam.

In Pehtia, the Ahrari family, including Waheedullah Ahrari, resided until they all migrated to Pakistan. Waheedullah Ahrari, a local schoolteacher, gained significant renown for his strong disapproval of British rule. He consistently raised his voice against the injustices of the Raj, leading to multiple imprisonments. He actively participated in various independence movements, never missing any uprising. Waheedullah Ahrari played a prominent role in civil disobedience, sharing a jail term with Pandit Nehru at one point. Additionally, he served as the secretary of the Khilafat committee. Despite being a distant relative in our family tree, I have heard numerous accounts of his courageous resistance, patriotic endeavours and fearless crusade against the Raj.

Waheedullah Ahrari was not only a vocal activist against British rule but also a talented artist. He worked at the university picture gallery and even created a portrait of Sir Syed. A pioneer in establishing Muslim guesthouses in Aligarh and Ghazipur, he continued serving the community after his government service. Despite someone misplacing his pension book out of spite, he chose to live his life without receiving a pension. Indira Gandhi acknowledged his services by awarding him the Tamir Pitr. Additionally, he was a skilled poet who used the pen name "Sahib" and composed poetry in the style of Akbar. A devoted disciple of Sheikh-ul-Hind Maulana Syed Hussain Ahmed Madni, he left an enduring legacy. Visiting Pehtia naturally brought back memories of this remarkable individual. In Karachi, his grandson Afzaal Bhai resides, and he was sure to inquire if I remembered his grandfather during my trip. Indeed, I did.

I don't think my feet had ever touched the ground in Pehtia before. Maybe I might have visited in the arms of my mother and thus my connection to the place. The profound, undeniable connection, however, was that my elders were from here and I loved this place for that very reason.

I am not sure that the entrance that got us into Pehtia was the only way in or if there were other entrance points as well. I was not familiar with the coordinates. When we arrived, I saw a Mazar where many Hindu pilgrims sat outside in scorching heat, praying for miracles. The heat could not dissuade or disturb them as they diligently concentrated in their prayers. Some kids, however, did rush to welcome us. It seemed as if it was a long time since a car had last driven up there.

This village had clearly seen better days, and most certainly that would have been around the time when my forefathers called this place home. The village was in a dismal state now.

Without any reservation, these people were generously showing us around their homes, or what remained of it. Many had missing pillars or roofs. The expensive stones and marbles had been taken out of the properties that had once belonged to us. What remained were dilapidated structures, ruined partly by the hard weather and partly due to loss of their original owners and no efforts to maintain them by the subsequent occupants.

I met a person sitting around wearing a tattered vest and looking almost as ruined and prehistoric as the ruins of the buildings around him. He gave a narrative of the nearby properties. One was the Haleema Manzil, and the other was Muhammad Ali Manzil. These were the houses of my grandparents. Decades had gone by, but it felt extremely gratifying that despite the passage of time, their names were still current on the lips and hearts of the people there. Once I made my introduction, they immediately welcomed my link and connection. They actually complained that we had left them here all alone back then. They were complaining that now, they had nothing. I wanted to tell them that we did not leave by choice or skip town by selling our land or possessions, but I decided not to go down that rabbit hole.

They spoke of the fruit-laden gardens and prosperous farms that had gone barren after we had left. It is almost impossible for them to earn a living in this remote village, and they seemed to blame me and my elders. I kept quiet and did not challenge them, for when fate had taken us from the comfort of this village and they had become owners overnight, they had inherited prosperous assets. It was on their watch that all this has turned to dust, rust and ruins. I think they probably understood their part of the blame and shortcoming and failure but found it difficult to accept it.

I, however, did ask the man about his children. Around that time, a women came out from behind a pillar wearing a sari in pourbi style, which I had seen older ladies of our family wear. In Pakistan, Parsi women wear sari that ways now. Not sure who are the originators, though—Pourbi or Parsi.

He introduced her as his wife and called out to his kids to come and meet me. His voice rebounded through the ruins, and soon, the four tall built sons lined up. "Won't you ask their names?" he quizzed, almost with relish. I was thinking that these sons should have been the saving grace for their old parents and should have helped erase their misery and poverty, but it did not seem that they were interested in that task.

He introduced his sons. "Abdul Azeem. Abdul Aleem. Abul Hasan. And this is Hasan Abdullah." My eyes got stuck on the youngest, Hasan Abdullah, for he had the same name as my father. The others were incidentally named after my two grandfathers and one after my uncle.

MOIST-EYED

I spoke with a mixture of surprise and annoyance and asked why he named his sons after my family members. With immense calm, he said, "They were accomplished people, and we kept their names to honour and remember them."

I was a bit confused, for if my family was to be honoured, then at least effort should have been made to educate the progeny and have them follow in the footsteps of those they were attempting to honour. Devoid of any education, they were merely whiling away their existence. Their gripe was that my elders had either left for eternal abode or Pakistan. I wonder how many times they would have griped about that over the decades.

However, I did not voice my thoughts, for I was meeting them for the first time and possibly the last. What's the point of being miffed about this? It is not that they will change their names or do any decent work for the remainder of their lives. Soon, I was actually able to empathise with them and even mustered some respect for their innocence. Other than handing them some money that I had on me then, what else could I do? In some ways, I was actually indebted to them for the time they spent talking to me about people and places that I hold dearest.

Now that I was in Pehtia, a lot of its history was coming back to me. I then remembered a well which our forefathers had dug up a few hundred years ago, and my father had written a poem about it as well. My father's grandfather used to look after that well as if it was a member of the family. The well was called Bair Ali. My father's grandfather was Muhammad Ali, so it was probably named after or associated with his name.

I put the question about the possible existence of well to the same man in the tattered vest sitting in the ruins of my grandfather's properties. In a way, it was also a test to see how well he knew them or their history. Straight off the bat he said, "Hasan Abdullah, take her to the well."

I was surprised, but I challenged him how I could be sure it was the same well I was talking about. He said the well still bore the plaque with the name Bair Ali on it.

Over, up and down shrub infested dirt pathways, I almost raced towards the well, with the young Hasan Abdullah leading the way. I was feeling blessed that the well had very timely surfed up in my memory at that time.

Hasan Abdullah got me to the well. The parapet wall was still intact, with some steel grills around it. I was surprised that the steel grills hadn't been uprooted and sold off as scrap, as is common in poor locales. Did steel have no value here?

After removing some shrubbery and dirt, I found the plaque, and lo and behold, it clearly read Bair Ali.

The founder of this well, whose name had traversed through time to us, was a certain Rahimullah, who was a very pious and religious man, immersed in the love of Allah and His Prophet Muhammad (PBUH). He had dug up the well to help the weary travellers and nearby communities and most certainly would have found his way to Jannah. A few centuries later, Hafiz Muhammad Ali adopted it and repaired it, and the sweet water helped satisfy the needs of the entire village. When he passed away, most certainly to Jannah as well, my grandfather carried the mission further and put a name plate on the well. And this is how the well came to be identified for the future generations.

My father, from this very village, went to Ghazipur and then went on to live in Aligarh. His act of writing a poem about the local well here had made it possible for me to be aware of its existence, and fate had brought me to it a hundred years after the name plate was placed there.

I peeked into the well. It was now filled with weeds and shrubs. Water probably dried up when the last of my family members, willingly or unwillingly, would have departed from here. They say when you peek in the well, you see your own reflection. However, I did not see my reflection. Instead, I did see those of my forefathers whose facial features I was not even aware of. I wished that there was water in the well so that I could drink that, and in that way, I could somehow have made that connection with the past. However, it had dried up. I sat on the stone ledge of the well. I touched the pillar and caressed my hands over the name plate. I wondered who had made the frame of the name plate and who would have carved the name on it. I wondered where the stones for the well would have been brought from and why their fate was destined for this well.

My getting here had been nothing short of a miracle, so I took a lot of pictures. At the well, I prayed fateha for my forefathers, for the well was nothing short of a lasting memorial. I sought apology from the well for coming so late. I peeked inside one last time before I left. Tears welled up, and I think some fell in the well as well. "Keep my tears safe dear well, for these are genuine tears that have travelled a very long distance of time and journey to get here."

Wells are made to benefit mankind. The founder will get the benefit for posterity, and those that came after him would have received benefit for keeping the tradition alive. I was from the fifth or sixth generation. I raised my hands and prayed, "My Allah, thanks to the good deeds of my elders, bless me as well."

Maybe the prayer reached the Heavens instantly, as I felt immense peace and calmness. I assumed this to be the outcome of my prayer.

In Pehtia, I was also saw Fatima Manzil. While it did not have a name plate, people around there, both Muslims and Hindus, in equal measure assured me that it was indeed Fatima Manzil. Surprisingly, it was in relatively good shape.

I asked a person standing in front of the house, wearing only a loin cloth, "Who does this house belong to?"

"This is my house," he replied calmly.

MOIST-EYED

"Do you know to whom it belonged to previously?" I queried.

He said it had been called Fatima Manzil for almost forever, but the farthest back he can remember is that it belonged to some jewel trader who left this place some hundred years ago. I did some mental calculations to try to connect the dots.

Sitting down to catch my breath on the roadside platform outside the house, I then told him that it was my paternal aunt's house. Her name was Fatima, and she was as beautiful as her name. She had even lived for a while in Karachi. My uncle, to whom the man was referring as a jeweller, was actually a perfumer. His name was Junaid Alam. Even today, his perfumery business is flourishing in several countries around the world, though Fatima or Junaid Alam are no longer alive. He was listening to me in rapt attention.

"Can I look inside?" I inquired, pushing my luck.

He happily agreed. "It's your own house. Come." He had no qualms in stating or agreeing to my ownership of the house.

"Why did you not change the name of Fatima Manzil?" I queried.

"Fatima is a blessed name," he replied as a matter of fact.

I was surprised that he knew Muslim history and that Fatima indeed was a blessed name of a very blessed and beloved personality in Islam. On the entrance door was the picture of three idols. "I have placed this, so people know we live here."

He pointed me to read what was written above the three idols. It was *Ayat-al-Kursi*. He said, "We have let it remain there, as they are blessed verses."

I did not sense a shred of bigotry in the talk of this Hindu occupant of my forefather's property. I looked at him with profound appreciation.

He was insistent on according hospitality. He wanted me to stay to eat and drink. "You have come after such a long time to your paternal aunt's house, so consider me your brother."

Who could say no to such genuine hospitality, but how could I tell him I and the next generation of my aunt live in the same city and we rarely get to meet. It is not that there is any love lost, but it's just our inabilities to prioritise our times. Anyway, this was not something to share with him. It was only for me to feel and be embarrassed about. I profusely thanked him for his hospitality and generosity.

Taking cue from the paucity of time, I sat back in the car and took off for the house of my uncle Dr Abdul

MOIST-EYED

Aleem. His family had shifted to Aligarh and did not opt to go to Pakistan.

Dr Abdul Aleem had gone on to become the vice chancellor at the illustrious Aligarh Muslim University, and I had seen his final resting place at the graveyard there. His grave was quite prominent and easily visible and was in the illustrious company of Aal Ahmed Saroor, Moeen Ahsan Jazbati, Zaheeruddin Alvi, Mumtaz Jehan and others. Only finding my own father's grave had been a gruelling task.

I soon found out that his house is now under Indian Government's control. There was no point of trying to understand the legality of the actions of Indian Government's annexation of the property

I also got to see the mosque of Pehtia that miraculously still sends out a call to prayers.

Back in the car, my mind was entangled in visualizing the old Pehtia. Those beautiful people in my family tree who I had never met, saw or knew, seemed walking all around me in Pehtia. The mansions seemed full of furniture and people and abuzz with richness of life and sounds. Courtyards laden with mango and guava trees, blackberry crates and other fruits and vegetables. Wheat and barley basking in the sun in large utensils. My imagination was so vivid, as if I had lived there and seen all the seasons and weathered the winters, spent the summers, the autumnal sadness and the spring bloom.

Back in the car, I also realised how hot it had been outside: 48°C. I hadn't noticed until then, for at that time, I was in a season beyond the four seasons. I do not know how to name that fifth season. Then I realised that it maybe was the season of pain. For my entire body was aching—physically and mentally.

My willpower was the only tonic that kept me going.

8

The history of migration and across-the-border relationships is so devastating that it blinds the eyes, and even pens cry on writing those stories.

Chapter 8

In the Courtyard of my Mother's Childhood

On the return journey, there was a stop at my mother's ancestral place—Muhammadabad. It was also the birthplace of my cousin sister Bilquis, who was my invaluable guide and generous host throughout this trip. This is where she was born, studied and wed, until she got posted to another city. She was quite glad to be going back to her maternal village, and I was delighted because I was getting a chance to go to my mother's maternal village.

This village, Muhammadabad, is also known as Yousufpur or Saleempur. Here, the Ansari and Hashmi families used to live. My mother was a Syed Zaadi of Hashmi lineage. My maternal grandfather was a learned and famous hakeem and had an incredibly well-respected practice and presence there. My mother was the sister to two brothers. Her brothers always tried to protect her share of anything and give it to her, but she was never keen for worldly possessions and used to distribute away whatever came her way, amongst the needy of this village. I had heard so many stories about the village, and I felt extremely excited to be here—the village of my grandparents and great-grandparents and the generation before them. I had finally arrived to meet them, but it was obviously quite late, for they all had left for their permanent abode.

It was so frustrating that when after so long, I did manage to make the pilgrimage to retrace my roots, all that was left to see were dilapidated, soulless houses. These lands and houses, although mine, were not the same. The owners and residents had been replaced. Courtyards and hallways were deserted, and rooms seemed to have somehow shrunk in size.

It was almost an hour-and-a-half-long journey getting into Saleempur. It was summer at its most inconvenient peak, but that did not deter me one bit as I looked outside from the car window in rapt amazement. Never in my wildest dreams had I thought that I would be making this commute to my mother's village and this road would come under my feet.

My mother's village map was very sketchy in my mind. My grandmother's face I could not recollect beyond a mere silhouette. However, I do remember that when we used to go from Ghazipur to Saleempur, my grandmother was always waiting for us. We used to get to enjoy the village produce. In summers, we used to drink sattu, and in winter, pure ghee balls, which we ate with delight. Suddenly, a long-lost, forgotten taste came back in my mouth. My grandmother used to add one spoon of pure ghee while cooking rice, which doubled the delightful taste. Taste and recipes were unique to my grandmother's house. I never found similar flavours anywhere ever again. In the evenings, at her house, we used to get roasted grams. That too was unique to her house.

As we covered ground and got closer to the Saleempur village, I remembered that my ears and nose were first pierced at my grandmother's house. She was the first one to put a silver earring in my ear. I also remembered a long-forgotten act of sliding a strand of the neem leaves into the nose piercing, as it helps contain inflammation. For years, I wore a nose piercing, but then at some point in time, I took it off, and the piercing filled up. I caressed my nose, as a long-forgotten memory had come to the fore.

I never got to see my grandfather. He died before I was born. My grandmother stayed back in India after the partition. She passed away on a date that was the day of Hajj-e-Akbar. I am told that when my mother met her for the final time before leaving for Pakistan, she cried a lot. I guess we siblings would have looked around in confusion as to why she was crying so much. My grandmother was in the process of bidding farewell to her only daughter, whom she loved dearly, and while she wished her good luck wherever she lived, she knew that she would probably never see her daughter again. And that is exactly what happened. In Pakistan, we got to hear of my grandmother's death back in India. My mother cried for so long on my grandmother's passing away that she fell so ill that she required medical treatment. She developed high fever, and we used to put wet towels on her forehead.

From my maternal grandfather's side, we had also said goodbyes to two uncles, two aunts and their children. Both uncles had a daughter each, similar to my age, who were our cousins and our best friends. We left them all behind and only got to hear of their passing away one after another over the decades. I could not even recollect most of the faces anymore.

When I arrived in Saleempur, the sudden thought of my mother grieved me intensely, and tears poured out. I stood in front of whatever remained of the majestic courtyard that my mother had spent a very blessed and happy childhood. That courtyard had fallen into disrepair. The entire building was in ruins. Most of the original residents that formed the nucleus of the family had all passed away. One brother was living there with his wife and daughter. He met with such warmth and intensity that it truly ached my heart in a good yet sad way. Genuine relations had been orphaned at the altar of politics of Indo-Pak partition and caged behind political borders.

In Saleempur, it seemed the sun had nowhere else to shine. There was no electricity for hours, and while I was offered cold water, it did not help.

MOIST-EYED

We had a few hours, after which, we had planned to return to Azamgarh. In those few hours, I went out to the nearby cemetery to meet my grandparents, uncles and aunts. Unfortunately, there were no markers on graves, and thus, it was impossible to find any graves that I could associate with. There was one proper grave and was locally known as the President Sahab's grave, but there was no elder around to shed light on who the occupant might be. It might have been someone from the local government and could have even been our near or distant relative, but I had no way of finding out.

Back in those days, adjacent to my mother's house used to be a red brick mansion which was always mysterious. It was two or three storey high and must have had more than forty or fity rooms. In that small village, this was by far the biggest building. This belonged either to my mother's uncle, or maybe some other relative, who worked at some senior position in the Indian Government at that time. However, we never saw it occupied. Probably ghosts dwelled there. At least that's what we thought back then. There was talk that some treasure was buried there, but pockets of opportunistic excavations probably yielded nothing.

Some lands or buildings inexplicably always remain barren or vacant. In its time, it was the most beautiful building around, but it was vacant then, and it was vacant now. The outer wall of the mansion, while in ruins, still stood around trying to hold onto its former glory. One side wall looked into towards my grandmother's courtyard.

My grandmother's house had always remained occupied although the residents withered down and the sprawling land mass lost its prized neem and fig trees. Here I was, thinking that if I had this much land space to my disposal in Karachi, I would have put every inch and corner to good use. Alas, there was no one to tend to it here.

A short distance away from my grandmother's house is a mosque whose upkeep is still our family's responsibility. I do not know who built the mosque, but what we do know is that on the day of birth of my mother, my grandfather had gone to this mosque and sat and prayed there until the safe and happy news of the birth of my mother had come through. All those at the mosque prayed for prosperity and long life for my mother on her birth. She was definitely prosperous in the love she got from her household as the apple of everyone's eye in her home and, after marriage, got a husband with a fantastic pedigree and tons of good attributes. Prayers for her long life got answered, as she lived to ninety years, but her husband's household prayers probably fell short, because he lived for only forty years and left behind my mother and five children to mourn his death.

The interesting thing about my grandfather's house was that he kept a detailed log of day-to-day happenings. A lot of people used to keep a diary in those times, but my grandfather, I am told, was clearly obsessed. I had always dreamt of laying my hands on those diaries. Obviously, nobody held on to them.

If all those writing could somehow have made their way to me, I would have gotten to relive all those days and it would have been nothing short of a time travel for me. I would have very much liked that. I would have enjoyed reading about the neighbours, the issues with relatives, the mundane and the major events of those days. I think those diaries might have waited for me for a while, but I took a very long time in coming. I felt guilty for being a late comer.

Some great personalities from Saleempur come readily to mind.

Dr Mukhtar Ansari, Hakim Nabina and Garam Diwan were all born in this small village but shone brightly in the annals of history.

Dr Mukhtar Ansari, a philanthropist, was one of the founders of Jamia Millia Islamia University and was also a nationalist political leader who actively led the Khilafat Thereek. Hakim Nabina's achievements are well documented in the history books, and as the legend goes, when Garam Divan Sahab was in trance of Divine immersion, bread could be baked on his back. I had heard of these people from my mother and also read about them in books, and they all called Saleempur home.

On the journey back, my thoughts got stuck on migration.

The history of migration and across-the-border relationships is so devastating that it blinds the eyes, and even pens cry on writing those stories. The house that I was returning from was now reduced from a mansion to one room. All the land around was sans their rightful owners, and the only guardians on those lands were weeds, pointed shrubs and dense undergrowth.

My feelings were quite broken and torn apart. The children and some adults of the village who had gathered upon hearing of my arrival were there in front of me. We were in front of each other but unfamiliar to each other. Their ancestors and my ancestors were relatives, and through those relations and especially the fact that I was the daughter to the daughter of that village; that led all to meet with such warmth. However, there was a palpable sense of loss and sadness as well.

I lost my mother fourteen years ago. I wish I could have come here earlier and then gone back to tell her stories of my visit to her village. But then again, what stories were there to take back home. A dilapidated house? Barren land all around? Decaying gardens devoid of fruits, vegetables, grains? All paled in sadness? It felt as if the land had vowed never to be productive again. There were no more water chestnuts around or mangoes by the dozens. No whole-wheat, barley or pearl millets were around, despite once being synonymous with the place. I felt my mother's village teary eyed. I was teary eyed too.

MOIST-EYED

However, tears were the only treasure I had which I was spending freely and yet never running out of.

I also met a domestic helper of my mother, who came rushing upon hearing "Amma ki Bitiya" was there. He was a Hindu, and in extreme reverence, he touched my feet. His mouth was wide open in amazement, and in his eyes, I could see decades of memories, as if he was trying to find a glimpse of my mother in my face. The evening shades were drawing large, and slowly but surely, I was retracing my path away from my mother's ancestral village.

Here I was, leaving forever, because what really was left for me to return to?

9

Karachi was the city that had adopted me, and I had adopted it—a city that was now my most beloved. This is where I had learned to live and survive. This is where I had secured my education as well as dispensed knowledge to hordes of students over a forty-year career in education. This is the city which houses my alma maters—school, college and university. This is where I had braved many a challenge and passed many a trials and tribulations.

Chapter 9

Back to Delhi and Return to Karachi

On 31 May 2014, I was back in Azamgarh, at the house of my cousin and my incredible and extraordinary host Bilquis. With her meticulous planning and support in full motion, the next day, I was to return to Delhi via a train ride, for which ticket reservations had been judiciously done in advance. From Delhi, on 2 June, I was to fly back to Karachi. My time in India was slowly drawing to its unavoidable close.

Everything had worked like the precision of a finely tuned timepiece—at least until then.

I soon received information, though, through media reports, that my 2 June flight from Delhi to Karachi had been cancelled. The inevitable tensions at the Indo-Pak borders were rearing their ugly head yet once again. A 4 June flight that was to leave for Lahore was the only available option before flights between India and Pakistan were to cease indefinitely. It was extremely inconvenient news, as the alternative flight involved a five-hour transit in Lahore before my onward journey to Karachi. I did not realise then, but the disparity in permitted luggage allowance for international and domestic flight was to—inexplicably and unfairly—create headaches for me at the Lahore airport as well. It also meant having to scramble to arrange accommodation in Delhi for additional two days.

I, however, had no qualms about staying another two days in Delhi. This was an ideal opportunity to meet Prof Irteza Karim, whom I could not meet earlier. Without any hesitation, I signed up for the alternate flight that was offered, slated to leave for Lahore on 4 June.

At Bilquis house, her daughter-in-law Shagufta and her kids all showered me with immense love. Azam was my nephew but cared for me like a son. This was the first time I was meeting them, but they went over and beyond in taking care of me.

In the 1968 film *Ghar Piyara Ghar*, Mujeeb Alam lent his voice to the lyrics of Habib Jalib, and I was reminded of this soulful rendition, *Bujhe na dil, raat ka safar hai.*

With such a sinking feeling, I cut a lonely figure on the crowded train for the long journey from Azamgarh to Delhi. 'Miles to go before I sleep.'

As I looked outside the window from my seat, I noticed water droplets trapped between the train carriage dual windows. I wondered if they happened to be there by chance or choice. Chance, though, had made it

MOIST-EYED

possible for me to be there then on this journey, and I felt blessed and empowered.

It was a relatively warm night, but the temperature in the carriage was inexplicably cold. However, the warmth of the stay in Aligarh, Agra, Azamgarh, Ghazipur and the nearby villages that I had visited kept me great company as I relived all those moments on the canvas of my mind on the long train ride. It is probably why I didn't notice many train stations as the train sped through, because I was mentally elsewhere.

I was reminiscing the all-round generosity, love, respect, hospitality and warmth of welcome of Prof Saghir Afraheim, Mehr Ilahi Nadeem, Riaz Ur Rehman Sherwani, Hakeem Zille Rehman, all the teachers and students of Department of Urdu, of Maulana Azad Library, of Sir Syed House, at the office of Thezeeb-ul-Ikhlaq, of my guest house, of Hamida apa, of Saeed bhai and even the driver who was with us for days at a stretch. I was remembering all the homes I had been invited to and all the wonderful people I had met. The fragrance of Aligarh was fresh and alive in my memory. It had carved its mark in my heart forever.

I was remembering the generous welcome from the Principals of Agra College and St John's College and their college staff. I had walked in without any prior appointments and left with such generous reception. I was recollecting all the architectural wonders of Mughal era that I was fortunate to see in Agra, including the Taj

Mahal. And how could I ever forget the Aligarh Muslim University graveyard—the final resting place of my father, Hasan Abdullah.

The train chugged along at a decent speed, but it could not rival the pace of memories that were flooding my thoughts and keeping sleep at bay.

Despite my being awake for nights at end and the body completely exhausted from the hectic travel and harsh weather, I had no complaints. I was leaving a lot richer than the first time I had to migrate. I was leaving loaded with a lifetime worth of indelible memories to savour and cherish.

By late afternoon on 1 June, I was back at the Orient Hotel in Delhi.

Orient Hotel is in front of Jamia Masjid, gate number 1. Although this hotel is a bit far and out of the way from the airport, this is where I had stayed when I had first arrived from Karachi, and this was again my hotel now on the way back.

It was going to be at least a two-hour wait to secure a room, as there were no rooms immediately available for my preferred lower floor room allocation request.

I utilised the wait time to venture out to shop in nearby markets, but the intent was not to buy excessively. I had been gifted a lot of books, and they were going to eat into my luggage allowance, and I did not have much

MOIST-EYED

expectation from PIA to be as generous with my luggage allowance as they had been on my flight into India.

In any case, most of the stuff I saw was readily available in Pakistan. Gone are the days when while returning from foreign trips, we used to chase the Form-A to secure dollar allowances for duty-free shopping in Karachi. Those were indeed amazing times, and the duty-free allowances did help us immensely in furnishing our home with the best electronic equipments of those times.

A lot of our friends and colleagues came to our house to witness their first microwave, first sandwich maker, first dishwasher and first rice cooker in action. However, time flies. Now, not just us, but anyone can secure these appliances, without the need for a Form-A. Today, we can buy any equipment without caring much about duty-free allowances. However, there was an unrivalled element of joy back then when we had to balance shopping desires with limited financial resources. When we were able to save enough to spend on something on our wish list, we absolutely cherished it.

The Delhi bazaars were stocked up with interesting wares, but nothing really caught my fancy. I, nonetheless, bought some souvenir stuff that was lightweight for all my grandkids.

Back in the hotel lobby, I noticed there were two newspapers available—*Inquilab* and **Sahara**. News of my visit and pictures had been detailed in both these papers during my tour of Aligarh. Prof Saghir Afraheim had already shared newspaper clippings of those events with me.

While re-reading the newspapers back in the lobby, I was advised that my room was finally available for check-in. I had already provided them a copy of my visa earlier but had to do so again. As Pakistani nationals, apparently, there were additional security protocols to be met, especially detailing our particulars in a separate guest register, where our signature was taken upon check-in and check-out. Once in my room, I immediately contacted Prof Irteza Karim, who was keen to invite me to Delhi University.

Prof Karim had visited Arts Council Karachi a few years earlier to participate in our Annual Urdu Conference. I had watched, listened and enjoyed his participation and contribution during the four days of the event. On the last day of the conference, I had gotten a chance to speak with him in private. I had given him **Afkar-e-Hasan**, which was my attempt at publishing all the available writings of my father that I could collate, in one volume. My wish was that he would help place the book at the Aligarh Muslim University or his Delhi University library collection. At that time, I did not know if I would ever personally get a chance to visit India. The odds had been stacked against it all my life. Prof Karim had accepted the book and the task associated with it, with genuine earnest. Maybe that is why he remembered me.

Despite Delhi University being closed for the summer break, he had called up all the professors at the university's Urdu department. It was exceptionally kind of him. I got to meet many professors and truly enjoyed the conversations. This time again, I handed over some additional copies of **Afkar-e-Hasan** with a request to further add them to the library's collection. The warmth with which the department professors met me will remain etched in my memory forever.

While at the Delhi University, I also met the head of the Persian Department. A scholarly Hindu person—whose name slips my mind—helped prove how India continues to provide academic options in foreign languages.

The Delhi University campus is massive with several entrances and exits. The landscaping around the camppus is exquisite. After the great hosting at the Delhi University, Prof Karim drove me to Urdu Academy, which was not too far from the Delhi University.

The secretary of Urdu Academy, Anis Ahsan Azmi sahab welcomed me with unmatched and genuinely warm enthusiasm. He was the eighth secretary of the Urdu Academy, and the walls at the offices of the Urdu Academy detailed the names and pictures of all his predecessors.

The office was pleasantly cold and a welcome respite from the searing heat outside. Along with cold drink, I was served cold cucumbers, the likes of which I had encountered everywhere on this trip—be it offices, houses or roadsides.

I was truly enjoying the fact that *Afkar-e-Hasan*, my compilation and publication of my father's poetry, was finding reception at such illustrious institutions. My father had left the world without an opportunity to have any of it published. The verses had been tucked away in a small diary and loose papers, and with Allah's help, I had secured and given them a new lease of life. Better six decades late than never!

I was quite interested in learning more about the Urdu Academy. Anis Azmi sahab gave me ample time and readily shared details. He mentioned that Delhi has always had a front-line role in the growth of Urdu and its spread. In 1980, the then Prime Minister of India, Indira Gandhi, had announced the setup of Urdu Academy. The allocated budget was INR 50,000. He mentioned that presently, the Chief Minister of Delhi, Sheila Dixit, was the Chairperson of the Urdu Academy.

Urdu Academy's role in mainstreaming and progressing Urdu via programmes include monthly publications with two such magazines, *Aiwan-e-Urdu* and *Umang*, which collectively have a circulation in excess of 12,000 copies. The other important thing the Academy is doing is publication of books and to its credit has 169 of them. In addition, financial assistance is disbursed for scripts as well as monthly stipend of INR 5,000 as fellowship for senior authors.

Along with book exhibitions, many seminars, literary meetings and talk shows are also held regularly. One such event is Nayay Puranay Chirag, which generates a lot of buzz and active participation of authors. Other activities that fill up the roster include a regular drama festival, coaching classes and Urdu literacy centre, and a lot of work is also being done on Urdu drama. He also mentioned conducting programmes in close collaboration with many other cultural societies of Delhi.

The main library of the Urdu Academy is named Dar Al Shikoh Library. It houses over 38,000 books and more than 150 rare manuscripts. Many Delhi published newspapers are being preserved here for posterity. There is also an Urdu composing and short-hand centre available.

Prof Karim had meanwhile disappeared briefly after driving me to the Urdu Academy. For a second, I thought he had left, but for him to leave without saying goodbye did not add up. He was back soon enough. He had gone to the library and returned with Prof Rasheed Ahmed Siddiqui's landmark book titled *Ganjaha-e-Granmaya* to make an even more powerful personal introduction on my behalf. I remain grateful to him for showing so much respect for my father. He conceded that it was certainly overdue, and more research work was merited on my late father, Hasan Abdullah.

I profusely thanked Prof Irteza Karim and Anis Azmi for the great work that they are doing. I was thanking them not just from my side but on behalf of my late father as well. I promised to stay in touch with them.

After this visit, a car courtesy of the Urdu Academy was arranged to drive me out to Ghalib Institute. Ghalib Institute is on Ghalib Avenue in a beautiful building on Mata Sundari Lane. Dr Syed Raza Haider, Director of the Ghalib Institute, awaited my arrival.

He welcomed me with enthusiasm and immediately took me on a tour of the entire Institute, which is what I naturally wanted. There is a life-sized portrait and sculpture of Ghalib at the entrance that beckons all.

He stated, and I was aware of it, that the creation of Ghalib Institute was the brainchild of the third President of India, Dr Zakir Hussain. In 1969, during the year of Ghalib's centennial death anniversary, the then Indian Prime Minister Indira Gandhi appointed Fakhruddin Ali Ahmed as committee secretary. Thanks to the efforts of this committee in 1971, Ghalib Institute came into being. Today, it is managed by a trust and is an invaluable platform for hosting education, literary and cultural events. Fakhruddin Ali Ahmed went on to become the fifth President of India, and the Institute has a library named after him as well.

Ghalib Institute's biggest draw is its museum. The plaque at the entrance indicates Begum Abida Ahmed as the patron. The museum was inaugurated in October 1977 and does a tremendous job of shedding light and preserving elements from Ghalib's era. Hundreds of visitors come here every day. The museum in-charge is Yasmin

Fatima, who seemed to be putting her heart and soul into the job and was kind enough to bring out a guest register for me to pen my thoughts as well.

It is indeed a very well maintained and detailed museum preserving and showcasing Ghalib in all its glory. Knowing Ghalib, he would certainly have been pleased and approved of it. On top of the signboard of the museum was one of his popular couplet:

یہ نہ تھی ہماری قسمت کے وصالِ یار ہوتا
اگر اور جیتے رہتے یہی انتظار ہوتا

Not in my destiny to have a union with my beloved;
Had I lived more, I would have waited more.

And just next to that signboard was another celebrated couplet:

رگوں میں دوڑنے پھرنے کے ہم نہیں قائل
جب آنکھ سے ہی نہ ٹپکا تو پھر لہو کیا ہے

We are not convinced by running in the veins;
Until it drops from the eyes, it is not blood!

The museum has several paintings depicting Ghalib, and the museum walls were coated with his couplets. There are also paintings on canvas of his peer poets and renderings of mushairas from that time. The museum has an impressive collection of manuscripts and multitude of books written about Ghalib and his poetry.

As with any other museum dedicated to an individual; Ghalib's clothes, utensils, way of life and other things from that time are staged meticulously for a very informative and interesting tour. Postage stamps from his time and those issued subsequently to honour him are showcased as well. The ambience is such that one feels being transported back into the time of Ghalib. I clicked as many pictures as I could to relive these again in the comfort of my home.

Ghalib Institute also boasts of an auditorium, which I really liked. In here, they hold seminars and poetic symposiums, where not just Indian poets but poets from all over the world participate. Every December, the auditorium—I was told—also hosts a world-class seminar about Ghalib as well as for people from his era such as Momin, Zauq and Bahadur Shah Zafar. Research scholars and people from all over the world enthusiastically attend this annual event. Ghalib Award is given for Urdu prose, poetry, critique and drama. Also, there is a bi-annual publication called *Ghalib Nama.*

MOIST-EYED

Ghalib had once prophesised that he would be remembered for his Persian rather than Urdu poetry. He was quite mistaken on that front, as it is his Urdu poetry that has propelled him into the league of world-class poets with enduring appeal. In his time, his poetry was deemed unconventional, but standing here in Ghalib Institute, it was evident that he was certainly ahead of his time.

With some twenty-person support staff, Ghalib Institute seems to be ably run by the learned Dr Syed Raza Haider. I had noted down the names of the current committees and their chairs as well:

- Hum Sub Drama Committee Chairman
  – Prof S.R. Kidwai

- Seminar & Literary Events Committee Chairman
  – Prof Shamim Hanfi

- Publications Committee Chairman
  – Prof S.R. Kidwai

- Museum Committee Chairman
  – Muhammad Shafi Qureshi

- Library Committee Chairperson
  – Begum Varneer Ahmed

- Ghalib Nama Auditorium Board Chairman
  – Prof S.R. Kidwai

- Finance Committee Director
  – Prof S. R. Kidwai

- Building Committee Director
  – Pervaiz Ali Ahmed

- Award Committee Chairman
  – Muhammad Shafi Qureshi

Each committee comprises some four or five learned and dedicated people supporting the committee's initiatives. They all deserve a standing ovation for their love for Ghalib and their dedication to the cause.

After a great tour, it was time to take leave.

On the way out, I again met the portrait and statue of Ghalib. I conveyed my regards and also slipped in the news that I had visited his house in Delhi's Ballimaran, which exists to this day and reminds us all of him. The lane is narrow, and the house is small, but this was of his own choice. It is to the credit of the Indian Government that the house is preserved to this date. Otherwise, commercial interests have often bulldozed many other historical landmarks.

This was to be my last night in India.

After the Indo-Pak partition, with me being a few years old, my family had left India. We had left behind relatives, properties in many cities, money, jewellery, businesses, farms, gardens and institutions that we had seeded. We had left behind the graves of our relatives, most important of those being of my father, with only a gravestone to remind all of his presence.

MOIST-EYED

Those that had stayed behind, however, found no need to have my father's grave taken care of. They had usurped his worldly possessions without any qualms, though. However, for me, the only thing that mattered was whether my late father had as keenly thought of me as I had ached for him for over half a century.

How can I ever forget the time when I was frantically searching every grave trying to find my father's? Then, I had lost hope in the searing heat and had sat down in a corner and shouted, "Baba, why I can't find you, despite having waited for so long and travelled such a long distance. I know I have taken too long to return, but then you too left early without any notice. We became orphans for life. But your little girl, your daughter is here now. Why are you still out of sight? I am told you used to call me Nakhal-e-bagh Arzoo-e-dil. You also called me Queen Caroline Phillis Victoria. The same queen is here now."

Then I had stood and cried in that scorching heat for so long that it even melted the heart and eyes of the graveyard caretaker too. And it was when I had threatened "Do you want me to leave without meeting you?" that I had heard a voice. I don't know whose, because I don't remember my father's voice, but I doubt if it could be anyone else's.

The voice had said, "Continue. Move ahead."

I did take a few steps. Then the voice had stopped.

I had looked around in despair, but who could one ask for help in a graveyard? I could not bear to stand any more, as my feet were hurting, with the ground heat searing and burning through the shoe soles. I was quite bitten and scratched by the wild shrubbery around as well. I just collapsed down at an obscure, unkempt grave that was overflowing with weeds. The tombstone was mired in soot and dust. As I had been doing all day, I had reached out and tried to clear the weeds and the tombstone to see if this was the one grave that meant the world to me.

And it was!

My father had certainly heard my voice and had finally steered me to his grave. I had cried non-stop, for I was relieved beyond words.

"I am sure you also did not want me to go without meeting you."

I have narrated this incident to many to seek their interpretation. It was surreal.

Some people have told me that those in the graves can hear us, and they even reply, but we cannot hear them. If this is true, then my father did hear my voice, and I'm grateful for him recognising and welcoming me.

"You have always lived in me and always will. No prayer in my life has been uttered unless it began with a plea for your salvation. I can never forget this meeting with you."

MOIST-EYED

It was evening time, and I was still reliving that incident in my mind when the phone rang.

It was Shoaib. He is the nephew of my sister-in-law in Karachi. He was insisting that I visit their house.

"How is that possible? I have a flight out of Delhi tomorrow!"

However, he was not willing to let the opportunity pass, so despite being quite late in the day, I relented.

Shoaib and Amina met me with incredible warmth and love. Their house was quite far away from my hotel, but their locale was very nice. They had prepared dinner but a neighbour of Shoaib, who was Alig and a renowned doctor, also invited me to dinner, so food from two households was collectively lavished at one place. He was a typical Alig from head to toe and regaled us with anecdotes as we ate delicious food.

It was soon way past midnight, and Shoaib insisted I stay the night at their house, and in the morning, I could return to the hotel to collect my luggage and go directly to the airport. However, I wanted to go back to the hotel for the night. The commute back to the hotel from Shoaib's house was almost an hour. I am truly indebted to him as well as Doctor sahab's family for the hospitality.

Shoaib dropped me off at the hotel. Without love and respect, nobody does this for anyone. I was truly grateful.

Sleep was still lightyears away. I was leaving India in the morning, but this time of my own volition. The last time I had departed, after partition, I had no recollection of that journey. However, this time, I remembered each moment of my stay of past two weeks in the five cities of India. I remembered each person I had met. I could recollect each and every road, shops, stalls, the nameless faceless people walking on the roads, frail bearers of cycle rickshaw, labourers in the fields, all those half-built, half-torn down dilapidated buildings, educational institutes, madrasas, relatives, friends, my innumerable hosts, the scorching heat and the eerie silence of the graveyard.

In the morning, I checked out after signing my name in the register. Even the hotel attendants wished me the very best and bid me farewell me with immense warmth.

I came back to the same Delhi airport where I had first landed two weeks back from Karachi. The atmosphere at airports is usually the same world over. Be it Heathrow in London, Shannon in Ireland, Jeddah, Riyadh, Dubai or Karachi's Jinnah airport, I've seen a fair bit. People and flights are constantly arriving while many others are departing. Some come just to say farewell, while others come to embrace and welcome. Some faces are beaming with happiness in anticipation of the journey ahead, and others sad at the prospect of having to say goodbyes.

I handed over the last visa slip at Delhi airport and took a quick glance back. "Goodbye, Baba," was all I could muster.

MOIST-EYED

Sitting in the familiar comfort of the PIA airplane, I read **Ayat-al-Kursi** and closed my eyes. I was departing for Karachi, albeit via a Lahore transit/detour.

Karachi was the city that had adopted me, and I had adopted it—a city that was now my most beloved. This is where I had learned to live and survive. This is where I had secured my education as well as dispensed knowledge to hordes of students over a forty-year career in education. This is the city which houses my alma maters—school, college and university. This is where I had braved many a challenge and passed many a trials and tribulations. This is where I had found lifelong friendships to share my moments of happiness and despair. This is the city that gave me professors who not only gave me knowledge but also wisdom to live life. This is where my near and dear ones now live or had lived. One such person was my mother who left me and the city at the start of this century. This is the city where I can visit her grave whenever I want. In this city, I live in an apartment near the famous roundabout—Teen Talwar. It's called Noor Ghar, after my children's paternal grandfather. As luck would have it, my children have now migrated to foreign lands. We seem to have made peace with it.

My husband and I now live in this house. Maybe when we are gone, the children will return. Maybe with this book in their hand, they will feel the void of the departed. Maybe they will see my writing table with all the books and stationery strewn across. Maybe their hearts will beat just a little bit faster. Maybe they will see the pictures of our and their youth on the room walls. Maybe they will smile. Maybe they will cry.

I opened my eyes. I tried to rid the multitude of thoughts swarming my mind and looked around in the plane. This was our national airline, Flight PK 272, which was ready to take off for Lahore, and from there, I was to take another flight to my beloved city, Karachi. The airhostess sounded over the PA system. "Please fasten your seat belt, as we are about to take off."

Yes, I was now finally ready to come back home; of my own free will.

Sahir Ludhianvi was blessing his college with the below couplet, but I find it an apt prayer for my city Karachi as well.

دورِ خزاں میں بھی تری کلیاں کھلی رہیں

تا حشر یہ حسین فضائیں بسی رہیں

May your blossoms bloom even amidst the fall;
May till eternity the beautiful atmosphere endures.

www.ingramcontent.com/pod-product-compliance
Lightning Source LLC
Chambersburg PA
CBHW072053110526
44590CB00018B/3146